01603 773114

ail: tis@

KT-493-646

Popular

Guide to

Norfolk Place-names

by James Rye

B.A., M.Phil., Cert. Ed.

The Larks Press

Published by the Larks Press
Ordnance Farmhouse, Guist Bottom
Dereham, Norfolk NR20 5PF

July 1991
Reprinted 1993, 1997

ISBN 0 948400 15 3

Printed by the Lanceni Press, Garrood Drive, Fakenham.

CONTENTS

ACKNOWLEDGEMENTS

The author wishes to acknowledge his indebtedness to all the writers listed in 'Suggested Further Reading' at the back of this volume, but especially to Eilert Ekwall whose 'Oxford Dictionary of English Place-names' (O.U.P. 1960) is the chief reference work, material from which has been used by permission of the Oxford University Press. Thanks are also due to the publishers for editing and supplementing the text.

PART ONE

Discovering Place-Names

Norfolk place-names can give us a wealth of **information, yet** at the same time they leave us asking questions. Who was first bitten so often that a modern family park became known as 'Gad-fly island'? Why were the weather conditions in a particular place so habitually bad that it became known as 'Cold shelter'? What happened to the birds of prey that were once so common in a popular holiday resort which was named after them? Who was the woman Ælswith who left an impression on a small community near King's Lynn? But each name has a story to tell, even though it may not tell us all that we want to know.

Perhaps in your mind 'Cromer' has always been a holiday resort, 'Sandringham' a place where the royal family has an estate, and 'Mulbarton' the place where you went as a child to visit Aunt Maud. It has never occurred to you that these words actually mean something. But the names didn't happen just because the first people to use them liked the sound that the words made. Our ancestors chose the names carefully to describe the people, wildlife, or countryside where they lived.

A Variety of Meaning

Place-names can give up to three main types of information. They sometimes tell us about the people who originally settled in the area. They often indicate, in general terms, what kind of settlement it was. And they frequently give us information about the natural world surrounding the place.

1

Folk Information

Many place-names are derived from the person or group of people who first settled in the area. For example, **Sweden** literally means 'the Swedes'. A less obvious example is **Wales**. This came from an Old English word *wealas* which meant 'foreigners'. To the early Anglo-Saxon invaders, Wales became the place of the foreigners after the invaders had driven many of the original Celtic inhabitants westward. **Wessex** was the area where the West Saxons lived. **Norfolk** is where the Northern People lived. The Southern People inhabited **Suffolk**.

The names of some of the towns and villages of Norfolk are also a memorial to people who travelled from the Continent, some as early as the fifth century, to cut the forests and attempt to make a living out of the land. The earliest of these names usually end in *ing* which is derived from the Old English *ingas* and originally meant 'dependants or relatives' of a certain man.

Blickling   Blicla + ingas, the settlement of Blicla's people

Gissing   Gyssa + ingas, the settlement of Gyssa's people

Sometimes these names end in *ingham* or *ington*. This is because *ham* or *tun* meaning 'homestead' and 'enclosure' respectively (see below) have been combined with *ingas*. The result is *ingaham* or *ingatun* meaning 'the homestead/enclosure of the people of...'

Dersingham   Deorsige + ingaham, the homestead of Deorsige's people

Islington   Elesa + ingatun, the enclosure of Elesa's people

Habitation Information

Many place-names contain an element meaning something like 'farm, homestead, enclosure'. As the settlements grew in size the same elements came to mean something like 'village' and later on even 'town'.

ham	first meant 'homestead'.
tun	first meant 'enclosure' or even 'fence'. Later it came to mean 'enclosure round a homestead, a farm' and then 'village'.
by	meant a 'homestead' or 'village'.
thorpe	usually meant a secondary or outlying farm attached to some other settlement.

These words meaning 'some form of habitation' were combined with a variety of other elements to give more precise information about the place.

Colby	Koli + by, Koli's village
Gayton Thorpe	secondary settlement attached to Gayton
Rougham	ruh (rough) + ham, uncultivated homestead
Santon	sand + tun, farm with sandy soil

Nature Information

Some place-names give information about the natural features of the area. We find references to a range of things including animals, birds, insects, crops, trees, bushes, streams, fords, landing-places, mounds, hills, valleys, ridges, meadows, woods, clearings, marshes, and islands.

3

Much of the original fauna has long since vanished. The far-
ming practices have changed. The woods have been cleared. The
marshes have been drained, making the islands disappear, and the
streams may have dried up or changed course. Only a few hills
retain an obvious link with the past for the modern visitor. The
natural world of the County that we drive through today would
not be recognisable to the Anglo-Saxon or Scandinavian settlers.
However, the place-names they have left us with are a kind of
time-capsule which reveals secrets of what the traveller would
have seen between a thousand and fifteen hundred years ago.

Cromer	crawe + mere, crows' pond
Feltwell	felte + well, stream where felte plants grew
Roydon	ryge + dun, rye hill
Sall	salh + leah, sallow wood

A Variety of Sources

British place-names contain elements that can be traced back to
the languages spoken by at least five quite distinct groups of
people. Some of us may have been misled by the victory in World
War II into thinking that Britain never has been 'slaved'. However, the truth is very different from what we may want to think.
The Welsh, the Scots, and the Irish are well aware that they often
have been invaded by the English (amongst others). And a brief
excursion into English history will reveal that the country has been
invaded by the Celts, the Romans, the Anglo-Saxons, the Scandinavians, and the French. All these people contributed words
which make up the place-names we have today.

The Celts

The Celts were one of the many tribes living in Europe in the years before Christ. About 400 BC they began to leave Central Europe, possibly because of harassment from other tribes. The Celts from Northern France and the Netherlands crossed the Channel and settled in England. They were known as *Brythons* (Britons). Later, about 350 BC, Celts from Southern France settled in Ireland. They spoke *Goidelic* (Gaelic).

They left behind names that are found most abundantly in the North and West. They also gave names to many rivers. Celtic names are often found in isolated spots which suggests that more remote groups remained Celtic-speaking long after other groups had accepted the language of the Anglo-Saxons.

Celtic elements include:—

aber	mouth of a river
coombe	a deep valley
glen	a narrow valley
pen	a hill
tor	a hill

There are very few names in Norfolk which contain Celtic elements. Most of the Celts probably fled the area when the Anglo-Saxon invaders arrived along the Eastern coast. The place-names in Wales and Cornwall are predominantly Celtic. The river name **Ouse** is the Celtic word for 'water'. **Lynn** is derived from *llyn*, the Celtic word for 'lake'.

The Romans

After 300 years of calling the British Isles their own, the Celts were conquered by the Romans. Between AD 43 and 410, England was the north-west corner of the vast Roman Empire. Although the Romans occupied the country for over three centuries, they only left behind about 300 place names. This strongly suggests that the Roman administrators tended to use existing Celtic names.

The main Latin elements in place-names are:—

castra (-chester, -caster)	a Roman town, fort
colonia (-coln)	a settlement
porta (-port)	a gate
portus (-port)	a harbour
strata (Strat-, -street)	a Roman road

As with the Celtic elements, there are very few names in Norfolk that contain Latin elements. **Caister** is derived from the Latin *castra*, and this element forms the second part of **Brancaster**.

The Anglo-Saxons

The Angles, Saxons, and Jutes began to invade the British Isles in 449 AD. They came from Denmark and the coast of Germany and Holland. Over the next 200 years, they settled and gradually wiped out all traces of the Celts. The Anglo-Saxons named their new country *Englaland* (the land of the Angles) and their language was called *Englisc* (what modern scholars refer to as 'Anglo-Saxon' or 'Old English').

Most place-names in Norfolk were originally given by the Anglo-Saxons. The Old English words that they used in place-names are far too numerous to list here. I have given a few of the common Old English place-name elements below.

bnrna (-borne)	a brook, stream
dun	a down, hill
eg (-ey)	an island
halh (-hall)	a corner, nook
ham	a homestead
hamm	a water meadow
ingas (-ing)	the people of ...
leah (-ley)	a clearing
stede	a place, site of a building
tun	an enclosure, farm
well	a well, spring
worth	an enclosure, homestead

Cantley, Downham, Tittleshall and **Wellingham** are good Norfolk examples of Old English place-names.

Cantley	Canta + leah, Canta's clearing
Downham	dun + ham, hill village
Tittleshall	Tyttel + halh, Tyttel's nook
Wellingham	well + ingaham, homestead of the people by the stream

The Scandinavians

From 789 AD onwards, Vikings from Denmark and Norway raided most parts of the British Isles. After much savage fighting they eventually settled down to live alongside the Anglo-Saxons. Modern Yorkshire, Derbyshire, Lincolnshire, Leicestershire, Norfolk, and Suffolk were taken over by the Scandinavians and became known as the *Danelaw*, that is, an area subject to Danish rule. The Scandinavian language, 'Old Norse', had the same Germanic

7

roots as Old English so, over the years, the two languages mixed quite well.

One of the interesting things about Norfolk place-names is that the County has a mixture of both Anglo-Saxon and Scandinavian names. Although Anglo-Saxon names predominate and the density of Scandinavian names is less in Norfolk than in parts of Yorkshire, it does have more Scandinavian names than counties such as Wessex.

Some of the common Scandinavian elements are listed below, although, as with the Old English elements, the Old Norse list does not claim to be anywhere near comprehensive.

by	a farm, then a village
dalr (-dale)	a dale, valley
garthr (-garth)	a yard
gil	a ravine
holmr (-holm)	flat ground by a river
lundr	a grove
thorpe	a secondary settlement, farm, small village
thveit (-thwaite)	a meadow
toft	a site of a house and outbuildings, a plot of land

In Norfolk, many of the Scandinavian names tend to be personal names followed by a habitation element.

Bowthorpe	Bo + thorpe, Bo's farm
Herringby	Hærringr + by, Hærringr's village
Tyby	Tidhe + by, Tidhe's village

The Norman French

The Normans invaded in 1066 AD, with the result that the

language of the English Parliament was French for the next 300 years. However, like the Romans, they left a very small legacy of place-names. This is because many of the settlement names would have been well established by the time of their invasion. Their presence in Norfolk can occasionally be glimpsed in modern distortions of the names of foreign lords who may have owned land on both sides of the Channel. For example, the **Toney** part of **Saham Toney** reflects the fact that the land was owned by the family of a certain Ralph de Toeni, standard bearer of William I, just after the Norman occupation.

Proceed with Care

Although driving through lanes trying to guess the meaning of the names on the sign-posts can be very entertaining, it is not always too productive. Even if you know that -*ham* is probably derived from the Old English word meaning 'homestead', you would not necessarily be able to say for certain that **Bradenham**, for example, meant 'something plus homestead'. This is because the Old English *hamm* (water meadow) also comes out as 'ham' in modern place-names. Only by looking particularly at early forms can you distinguish between the two, and even then, it is not always possible. In this particular case, **Bradenham** could mean either 'broad river meadow' (*brad* + *hamm*) or 'broad homestead' (*brad* + *ham*).

Until the early spelling of a particular name is known (and by 'early' I mean at least the twelfth century or before), it is not possible to see clearly which Celtic, Old English, Old Norse, or even Old French elements went to make up the name. Place-name scholars have to hunt through a variety of historical documents in order to record the early spellings. The most famous of these sources are Bede's *History of the Church* and the *Domesday Book*.

Let me illustrate the importance of knowing something of the history of the spelling of a particular name before making over-confident pronouncements about meaning. I have taken four Norfolk places to demonstrate my point: **Hautbois, Fiddlers Dykes, Kimberley** and **Middleton.**

When I first became interested in place-name study I rashly concluded that **Hautbois** must mean 'high wood'. From my limited knowledge of French I knew that *haut* meant 'high' and *bois* meant 'wood'. What could be simpler! However, in my naivety I had yet to learn that French names are rare, and that modern forms often differ quite radically from early spelling. In fact **Hautbois** means 'meadow with tussocks or by a hummock'. Early forms of the name are *Hobwiss* and *Hobwise* and show that it is derived from two Old English words *hobb* 'a tuft of thick grass, or a hummock' and *wisce*, 'a marshy meadow'.

For the uninitiated and romantic, **Fiddlers Dykes** conjures up pictures of a Traveller serenading the community. Leaving aside the issue that violins are a relatively late invention, **Fiddlers** der-ives from the fact that the family of John Vis de Lu (wolf-face) held the area in 1248. At the time *f* was often pronounced as *v*, and there was considerable confusion in the spelling of words which had these letters at the beginning. Words beginning in *v* could be spelt with an *f*. Thus, over time, *Vis de Lu* became 'Fiddlers'.

Two more examples show the need to proceed with caution before making hasty judgments about meaning. There is a **Kim-berley** in Norfolk, one in Nottinghamshire, and one in Warwick-shire. One could be forgiven for thinking that they all meant the same. However, such an assumption would be wrong. Their early spellings reveal that the three settlements were founded around three people having quite distinct names.

Norfolk	*Cyneburg* + *leah*, Cyneburg's clearing
Nottinghamshire	*Cynemær* + *leah*. Cynemær's clearing
Warwickshire	*Cynebald* + *leah*, Cynebald's clearing

The Norfolk **Kimberley** is particularly interesting in that *Cyneburg* is a woman's name.

There are several settlements called **Middleton** throughout the country, but the early spellings again reveal that they can sometimes mean quite different things. The Norfolk **Middleton** is quite straightforward and means simply 'middle enclosure/farm'. However, the one in Herefordshire means 'large enclosure/farm' and the one in Shropshire means 'enclosure/farm in the clearing at the junction of two streams'.

Norfolk	*middel* + *tun*, middle enclosure
Herefordshire	*micla* + *tun*, large enclosure
Shropshire	*gemyth* + *leah* + *tun*, enclosure in the clearing at the junction of two streams

A knowledge of the geography of a particular area can also throw light on the meaning of the name. The Old English word *sæ* can mean 'a lake' or 'the sea'. Obviously when it occurs in inland places such as **Saham** it will mean 'lake' unless there is good reason to believe that the particular place used to be on the coast before land reclamation. **Lyng** could be derived from the Old Norse word *lyng* meaning 'heather'. However, a more acceptable explanation might be to trace it back to the Old English *hlinc*, meaning 'a bank or ledge'. The road north-east of East Dereham follows the course of the River Wensum, and is probably on a river terrace.

The Place-name List

In the second part of this book I have listed the meaning of over 600 Norfolk place-names. Where the experts disagree about a meaning, or where there is a degree of doubt, I have tried to indicate that in my text. Where a place is recorded in *Domesday Book* the spelling (or one of the spellings) that is used there is given in italics below the main place-name entry.

Abbreviations

CE	Celtic
DB	Domesday Book
H	Hybrid (a name containing elements from both Old English and Old Norse.)
L	Latin
OE	Old English
OFr	Old French
ON	Old Norse

PART TWO

Place-names of Norfolk

Crops, Plants and Trees

Acle
Acle
Oak grove. OE *ac* (oak) + *leah* (wood, grove, clearing).

Alderford
Alrelie
The ford at the alder trees. OE *alor* (alder) + *ford*.

Appleton
Appletuna
Enclosure with apple trees. OE *æppel* (apple tree) + *tun* (enclosure, settlement, farm).

Ashby
Essebei
Village where ash trees are common. H. OE *æsc* (ash) + ON *by* (settlement, village).

Ashill
Asscelea
Ash grove. OE *æsc* (ash) + *leah* (wood, grove, clearing).

Ashwell Thorpe
Torp
Ash stream secondary settlement. OE *aesc* (ash) + *well* (stream) + ON *thorpe*. About 1066 eight acres of land were conveyed to Ashwell church.

Ashwicken
Wiche
Dairy farm by the ash trees. OE *wicum* (at the dairy farm) + *aesc* (ash).

Bale
Bathele
Bath grove. OE *baeth* + *leah* (wood, grove, clearing). Some have suggested that the 'bæth' element may refer to warm springs. Others have argued that the wood provided timber suitable for making baths.

Banham
Benham
Homestead where beans are grown. OE *bean* + *ham* (homestead).

Barford
Bereforda
Barley ford. OE *baerlic* (barley) + *ford*.

13

Barney
Berlei

Either barley or barn island. OE either *beren* (of barley) or *berern* (barn) + *eg* (island).

Barton
Bertuna

Barley farm or outlying grange for storing crops. OE *beretun* (originally a 'threshing floor', then a 'corn farm', and then 'an outlying grange for storing crops'.) **Bendish** means 'inside the ditch', OE *be innan dic*. The place is west of Devil's Ditch. **Turf** indicates a place where good turf was found.

Barwick
Berewica

Barley farm or outlying grange. OE *berewic* (corn farm). See **Barton.**

Bastwick
Bastwic

Farm where bast (inner bark of lime) is obtained, or farm in a lime grove. OE *baest* (bast) + *wic* (farm).

Beeston
Besetuna

Sedge or bent grass enclosure. OE *beos* (sedge or bent grass) + *tun* (enclosure, settlement, farm).

Beetley
Betellea

Possibly grove from which wooden mallets were obtained. The second element is OE *leah*. The first element may be OE *bietel* (beetle, mallet).

Bixley
Bichesle

Box-wood grove. Almost certainly identical with **Bexley.** OE *byxe* (box wood) + (wood, grove, clearing).

Blofield
Blawefelda

Possibly open ground with woad plants. OE *blaw* ('blue' in the sense of 'pigment made from woad plants') + *feld* (open ground).

Bracon Ash
Braccles
Bracondale

Bracken and ash trees. OE *bræcen* or ON *brakni* (bracken) + OE *æsc* (ash trees)

Bracken valley. OE *bræcen* or ON *brakni* (bracken) + OE *dael* or ON *dalr* (valley).

Bramerton *Brambretuna*	Enclosure among the brambles. OE *bremer* (brambles) + *tun* (enclosure, settlement, farm).
Brampton *Brantuna*	Broom enclosure. OE *brom* (broom) + *tun* (enclosure, settlement, farm).
Brancaster *Broncestra*	Broom camp. 960 *Bramcestria*. OE *brom* (broom) + *ceaster* from L *castra* (camp).
Brandon *Brandun*	Broom hill. OE *brom* (broom) + *dun* (hill).
Bromholm	Broom island. OE *brom* (broom) + *holm* island.
Broome *Brom*	Place where broom is abundant. OE *brom* (broom).
Brumstead *Brnmestada*	Broom-covered place. OE *brom* (broom) + *stede* (place.)
Brundall *Brundala*	Broomy nook. OE *brom* (broom) + *halh* (nook or corner of land).
Bunwell	Spring with reeds. OE *bune* (reed) + *well* (spring, stream*)*.
Dilham *Dilham*	Homestead where dill is grown. OE *dile* (dill) + *ham* (homestead).
Docking *Dochinga*	Place where docks grow. OE *docce* (dock, water-lily).
Elmham *Elmenham*	Elm homestead. OE *elm* + *ham* (homestead).
Feltwell *Feltwella*	Possibly stream where the felte plant grows. The second element is OE *well* (stream). OE *felt* occurs in some OE plant names, and there may have been a plant such as *felte*.
Fersfield *Fersuella*	Open land covered with furze (spiny, yellow-flowered evergreen shrub, gorse, whin). OE *fyrs* + *feld* (open land).

Flegg *Flec*	Possibly place of water plants or flags if the element is ON *flœg*.
Hempstead *Hemesteda* *Henep*	The one near **N. Walsham** simply means 'homestead', OE *ham* + *stede* (place). However, the one near **Holt** means 'place where hemp is grown', OE *henep* (hemp) + *stede*.
Hethel *Hethella*	Hill overgrown with heather. OE *hœth* (heather) + *hyll*.
Heydon	Hay hill. OE *heg* (hay) + *dun* hill.
Hockham *Hocham*	Settlement where hocks grow or Hocca's homestead. OE *hocc* (hock) or *Hocca* + *ham* (homestead).
Hockwold *Hocwella*	Wood/wasteland where hocks grow. OE *hocc* (hock) + *wald* (woodland, or later waste ground that had been cleared of trees.)
Letton *Lettuna*	Leek enclosure, or enclosure by a brook. OE *leac* leek or *lece* brook + *tun* (enclosure, settlement, farm).
Plumstead *Plumestede*	Dwelling site near the plums. OE *plume* (plum) + *stede* (place).
Redenhall *Redanahalla*	Possibly reedy nook. Probably the first element is OE *hreoden* (reedy). The second element is OE *halh* (nook, corner of land).
Reedham *Redaham*	Either homestead by the reeds, or reed meadow. OE *hreod* (reed) + either *ham* (homestead) or *hamm* (meadow).
Roudham *Rudham*	Possibly homestead where rue plants are grown. The second element is OE *ham* (homestead). The first element is probably OE *rnde* (rue plant).

Roughton *Rugutune*	Either rye or rough enclosure. The second element is OE *tun* (enclosure, settlement, farm). The first element could be OE *ruh* (rough). Or the name could be a hybrid, having ON *rugr* (rye) as a first element.
Roydon *Reiduna* (nr. Lynn) *Ragheduna* (nr. Diss)	Rye hill. OE *ryge* (rye) + *dun* hill.
Rushford *Rusceworda*	Ford with rushes. OE *risc* (rush) + *ford*.
Ruston *Ristuna*	Brushwood enclosure. OE *hris* (brushwood) + *tun* (enclosure, settlement, farm).
Ryburgh *Reieburh*	Fortified place where rye is grown. OE *ryge* (rye) + *burg* (fortified place).
Ryston *Ristuna*	Brushwood enclosure. OE *hris* (brushwood) + *tun* (enclosure, settlement, farm.)
Salhouse	Sallow willows. 1574 *Sallowes*. OE *salh* (sallow willows).
Sall *Salla*	Sallow wood. OE *salh* (sallow willows) + *leah* (wood, grove, clearing).
Sco Ruston *Ristuna*	Settlement in a brushwood wood. H. ON *skogr* (wood) + OE *hris* (brushwood) + *tun* (enclosure, settlement, farm).
Sedgeford *Sexforda*	Ford where sedge grows. OE *secg* (sedge) + *ford*.
Setchey	Possibly sedge-covered landing-place. 1291 *Sechyth*. Possibly *secg* (sedge) + *hyth* (landing place).
Sloley *Slaleia*	Blackthorn grove. OE *slah* (blackthorn) + *leah* (wood, grove, clearing).
Thornage *Tornedis*	Pasture where thorns grow. OE *thorn* + *edisc* (pasture).

17

Thornham *Tornham*	Homestead at the thorn trees. OE *thorn* + *ham* (homestead).
Thurne *Thura*	Thorn bush. OE *thyrne* (thorn bush).
Thurning *Tyrninga*	Either place where thorn bushes grow, or people at the thorn bushes. A derivative of OE *thyrne* (thorn bush). It is either *thyrne* + *ing* (place of ...) or *thyrne* + *ingas* (people of ...).
Thurton	Thorn enclosure. OE *thyrne* (thorn) + *tun*.
Wheatacre *Hwateaker*	Arable land used for wheat. OE *hwæte* (wheat) + *acer* (field).
Whinburgh *Wineberga*	Fortified place overgrown with whin (furze). The second element is *burg* fortified (place). The Middle English word *whin* is derived from the ON *hven*.
Wicklewood *Wikelewuda*	*Wicleah* Forest. OE *wice* (wych elm) + *leah* (wood, grove, clearing) + *wudu* (wood).
Wilby *Wilgeby*	Village in the willows. H. OE *welig* (willows) + ON *by* (village).
Wilton *Wiltuna*	Settlement in the willows. OE *welig* (willows) + *tun* (enclosure, settlement, farm).
Woodbastwick *Bastwic*	Bastwick Wood. Bastwick + *wudu* (wood) Cf. **Bastwick**.
Wretham *Wretham*	Homestead where crosswort (a medical plant) is grown. OE *wrætt* (crosswort) + *ham* (homestead.)
Wretton	Enclosure where crosswort (a medical plant) is grown. OE *wrætt* (crosswort) + *tun* (enclosure, settlement, farm).

See also **Hethersett, Lynford, Lyng, Ridlington**

Animals

Barmer
Benemara

Possibly bear pool. The second element is OE *mere* (pool). The first element may be OE *bera* (bear).

Buxton
Buchestuna

Buck deer enclosure. The first element may be a nickname. OE *buc* (male deer) + *tun* (enclosure, settlement, farm).

Catfield
Catefelda

Open land where wild cats are found. OE *catte* (wild cat) + *feld* (open land).

Dereham
Derham

Homestead where deer are found, or enclosure for deer. The name could be OE *deor* (deer) + *ham* (homestead). However, it is most likely to be *deor-hamm* (enclosure for deer.)

Foxley
Foxle

Fox wood/grove. OE *fox* + *leah* (wood, grove, clearing).

Gateley
Gatelea

Clearing where goats are kept. OE *gate* (goat) + *leah* (wood, grove, clearing).

Hethersett
Hederseta

Either heather fold or stag deer fold (probably the latter.). The first element is either OE *hæth* (heather) or *heahdeor* (stag deer). The second element is OE *(ge)set* (fold.)

Horsey
Horseia

Horse land surrounded by water. OE *hors* (horse) + *eg* (island.)

Horsford
Hosforda

Horse ford. OE *hors* (horse) + *ford*.

Horsham
Horsham

Enclosure where horses are kept. OE *hors* (horse) + *ham* (homestead).

Horstead
Horsteda

Place where horses are kept. OE *hors* (horse) + *stede* (place).

Lamas *Lamers*	Possibly lamb marsh. More probably loam marsh. OE *lam* (loam) or *lamb* + *mersc* (marsh).
Martham *Martham*	Homestead or water meadow frequented by martens (animals like weasels). OE *mearth* (marten) + *ham* (homestead) or *hamm* (water meadow). Cf. **Marlingford**.
Oxborough *Oxenburch*	Old fort frequented by oxen. OE *oxa* (oxen) + *burg* (fortified place).
Oxnead *Oxenedes*	Pasture for oxen. OE *oxna* (for oxen) + *edisc* (pasture).
Oxwick *Offuic*	Ox farm. OE *oxa* (oxen) + *wic* (farm).
Shipden *Scipedana*	Sheep valley. OE *sceap* (sheep) + *denu* (valley).
Shipdham *Scipdham*	Possibly homestead with a flock of sheep. The second element is OE *ham* (homestead). The first element is probably a derivative of OE *sceap* (sheep).
Stody *Stodeia*	Enclosure for horses. OE *stod* (a stud, herd of horses) + *gehæg* (enclosure).
Titchwell *Tigeswella*	Kid spring. 1035 *Ticeswelle*. OE *ticcen* (kid) + *well* (spring).

See also **Barsham, Catton, Haveringland, Marlingford.**

Birds and Insects

Anmer
Anemere

Duck pool. OE *æned* (duck) + *mere* (pool).

Bawburgh
Bauenburc

Gadfly fort. OE *beaw* (gadfly) + *burg* (fortified place). The first element is probably a nickname.

Bawsey
Boweseia

Gadfly island. OE *beaw* (gadfly) + *eg* (island). The first element may be used as a nickname.

Brisley

Gadfly glade. OE *briosa* (gadfly) + *leah* (wood, grove, clearing).

Cockley Cley
Claia

Place of clayey soil. 1574 *Clay*. OE *clæg* (clay). The additional **Cockley** is obscure. It may mean wood frequented by birds — possibly OE *coc* + *leah*.

Corpusty
Corpestig

A path from which many ravens can be seen. Possibly H. ON *korpor* (raven) + OE *stig* or ON *stigr* (path).

Coxford

The second element is *ford*. The first element could be *cocc* (wild bird), *cocc* (heap, hill) or *Cocca*. The first possibility is most likely.

Cranwich
Cranewisse

Cranes' marshy meadow. OE *cran* (crane) + *wisce* (marshy meadow).

Cranworth
Craneworda

An enclosure round a homestead where cranes are seen. OE *cran* (crane) + *worth* (an enclosure round a homestead).

Cromer

Crows' pond. 1574 *Crowmere*. OE *crawe* (crow) + *mere* (pond).

Doughton

Duck enclosure. OE *duce* (duck) + *tun* (enclosure, settlement, farm).

Fincham *Phincham*	Homestead frequented by finches. OE *finc* (finch) + *ham* (homestead).
Foulden *Fugalduna*	Hill frequented by birds. OE *fugol* (fowl) + *dun* (hill).
Foulsham *Folsam*	Homestead of the birds. OE *fugol* (bird) + *ham* (homestead).
Rockland *Rokelunda*	Rook grove. ON *hrokr* (rook) + ON *lundr* (grove).
Tivetshall *Teveteshala*	Lapwings' nook. OE *tewhit* (lapwing) + *halh* (nook, corner of land).
Wroxham *Vrocsham*	Either homestead where buzzards (birds of prey) are common, or ?*Wroc's* homestead. There may have been an OE word *wroc* which is similar to an old Swedish word *vrak* (buzzard). The second element is OE *ham* (homestead).
Yaxham *Jachesham*	Either cuckoos' meadow or *Geac's* homestead. The first element is either OE *geaces* (cuckoos) or it could be a personal name (?*Geac*). The second element is either OE *hamm* (meadow) or *ham* (homestead).

See also **Bressingham**, **Lexham**, **Wreningham**.

More about Land, Water, and Settlements

Bilney
Bilenei

An island on a beak of land. The first element is OE *bile* meaning 'a beak'. It could be a personal name, but it is more likely to be used in a topographical sense. The second element is OE *eg* (island).

Blo Norton
Nortuna

Possibly bleak/cold north enclosure. OE ?*blaw* + *north* + *tun* (enclosure, settlement, farm).

Breydon Water

Place where a narrow piece of water widens; a tidal mere (near the mouth of the Yare). H. ON *breithing* which became *bredding* (place where narrow water widens).

Burston

Possibly settlement by the landslip. OE *byrst* (landslip) + *tun*.

Caldecote
Caldanchota

Cold cottage/shelter. OE *cald* (cold) + *cot* (cottage).

Carbrooke
Cherebroc

Possibly dark stream. H. CE ?*cero* (dark) + OE *broc* (stream).

Carrow

Projecting rock hill-spur. OE *cæg* ('key' in the topographical sense of 'projecting') or OE *carr* (rock) + *hoh* (hill-spur).

Choseley

Gravelly grove. OE *ceosol* (gravel) + *leah* (wood, grove, clearing).

Cley
Claia

Place of clayey soil. 1574 *Clay*. OE *clæg* (clay).

Diss
Dice

Ditch or moat. OE *dic* (ditch, moat or embankment).

Drayton
Draituna

Enclosure by a portage. OE *dræg* (dray or portage) + *tun* (enclosure, settlement, farm).

Emneth	Smooth meadow, or junction of streams on the River Æmenan. OE *emn* (smooth) + *mæth* (meadow), or *Æmenan* (possibly an old name of the Nar) + *gemythe* (mouth, junction of streams).
Felbrigg *Felebruge*	Plank bridge. Possibly H. ON *fiol* (plank) + ON *bryggia* or OE *brycg* (bridge).
Flitcham *Flicham*	Homestead where flitches of bacon are produced. OE *flicce* (flitch) + *ham* (homestead).
Flordon *Florenduna*	Possibly tessellated-pavement hill. The second element is OE *dun* (hill). The first element *flor* is obscure. Gelling has argued the topographical sense given.
Gressenhall *Gressenhala*	Gravelly nook. OE *greosn* (gravel) + *halh* (nook, corner of land).
Hackford *Hacforda*	Ford at a river bend, or ford with a sluice grating to catch fish. The first element is either OE *haca* (hook, here in the topographical sense) or *hæcc* (flood-gate or sluice) + *ford*.
Hardley *Hardale*	Hard clearing (perhaps referring to the soil). OE *hard* + *leah* (wood, grove, clearing.)
Hautbois *Hobuisse*	Meadow with tussocks or by a hummock. Early forms are *Hobwiss*, *Hobwise*. (It is **not** French for 'high wood'.) OE *hobb* + *wisce*.
Heacham *Hecham*	Possibly a homestead with a hedge, or it may be a homestead with a grating to catch fish. The second element is OE *ham* (homestead). The first element is either OE *hecg* (hedge) or OE *hæcc* (sluice). Cf. **Hackford** and **Heigham.**

Heigham	Identical to **Heacham**
Houghton	Enclosure on a hill-spur. OE *hoh* (hill-spur)
Houtuna	+ *tun* (enclosure, settlement, farm). The new village was built c. 1729 to replace the old village of **Houghton** that was demolished to allow the construction of Houghton Hall 1722-35.
Irstead	Possibly muddy place. The second element is OE *stede* (place). The first element may be OE *gyr* (mud).
Keswick	Cheese farm. H. ON *kes* (cheese) + OE
Kesewic	*wic* (farm).
Lenwade	The second element is OE *gewæd* (ford). The first element has been the subject of considerable debate and is still uncertain. The name may mean 'ford of the slowly moving river'. Gelling suggests that the first element is *lone* in the Scottish dialect sense of 'scarcely moving river'.
Loddon	Loddon is an old name for the River Chet.
Lotna	The settlement came to mean dwellers by the River Loddon. Loddon meant 'muddy'. CE *lutna* (mud).
Lynford	Probably flax ford. OE *lin* (flax) + *ford*.
Lineforda	
Mileham	Homestead with a mill. OE *mylen* (mill) +
Meleham	*ham* (homestead).
Overstrand	Possibly narrow shore with a steep edge.
Othestranda	1231 *Ovestronde*. The second element is OE *strand* (strand/shore). The first element may be OE *other* (other), to distinguish **Over-**

Paston
Pastuna

Rackheath
Racheitha

Repps
Repes

Rougham
Ruhham

Runhall
Runhala

Runham
Ronham

Salthouse
Salthus

Santon
Santuna

strand from **Sidestrand**, or it may be OE *ofer* (edge, margin).

Enclosure by the small pools. OE *pæsc* (puddle, small pool) + *tun* (enclosure, settlement, farm).

The first element may be the OE word for throat (*hraca*) used in the sense of 'a gully' + *hyth* (landing-place). The name would mean 'landing-place near a gully'. **Rackheath** is 2 miles from the River Bure, but the 1" map shows a tributary of the Bure flowing past the church, and there may have been enough water in early times to form a small harbour away from the marshes which border the main river.

Strips of land in a fen that could be tilled. 1191 *Repples*. OE *ripel* (strip).

Rough (uncultivated) homestead. OE *ruh* (rough) + *ham* (homestead).

Possibly nook by the fallen tree. The second element is OE *halh* (nook, corner of land). The first element may be *hruna* (fallen tree, log).

Homestead by the fallen tree, or *Runi's* homestead. OE *hruna* (fallen tree, log) or ?*Runi* + *ham* (homestead).

House for storing salt. OE/ON *salt* (salt) + *hus* (house).

Enclosure on sandy soil. OE *sand* (sand) + *tun* (enclosure, settlement, farm).

Scarning *Scerninga*	Possibly dirty brook. The original word may be a derivative of OE *scearn* (dirt) which may have referred to a stream.
Shadwell	Boundary stream. OE *scead* (boundary) + *well* (stream).
Sharrington *Scarnetuna*	Muddy enclosure, dung enclosure. OE *scearn* (mud, dirt, dung) + *tun* (enclosure, settlement, farm). Cf. **Scarning.**
Shelfanger *Sceluangra*	Sloping wood on a shelf, pinnacle. OE *scylf* (shelf /pinnacle) + *hangra* (slope/sloping wood).
Shelton *Sceltuna*	Enclosure on a pinnacle or shelf. OE *scylf* (shelf / pinnacle) + *tun* (enclosure, settlement, farm).
Shereford *Sciraforda*	Bright (clear) ford. OE *scir* (bright) + *ford*.
Shernborne *Scernebrune*	Muddy stream. OE *scearn* (mud, dung) + *burna* (stream).
Shouldham *Sculdeham*	Possibly debt homestead, homestead that paid rent. The second element is *ham* (homestead). The first may be OE *scyld* (debt/due).
Sparham *Sparham*	Homestead or meadow with an enclosure. OE *spearr* (enclosure) + *ham* (homestead) or *hamm* (meadow).
Stanhoe *Stanhou*	Stoney hill-spur. OE *stan* (stone) + *hoh* (hill-spur).
Stiffkey *Stivecai*	Tree-stump island. OE *styfic* (stump) + *eg* (island).
Strumpshaw *Stromessaga*	Stump grove. OE ?*strump* (stump) + *sceaga* (small wood).

27

Swafield *Suafelda*	Open land characterized by swathes. OE *swæth* (ridges of grass or corn lying after having been cut) + *feld* (open land).
Taverham *Taverham*	Enclosure with red soil. OE *teafor* (red pigment) + *ham* (homestead).
Trowse *Treus*	Wooden house. OE *treo* or ON *tre* (tree) + OE/ON *hus* (house).
Trunch *Trunchet*	This may be a name transferred from France. Le Tronchet Abbey had possessions in Norfolk. Gelling argues that **Trunch** means 'wood on a promontory' and is a derivative of two CE words *tron* (nose) + *coid* (wood).
Twyford	Double ford. OE *twegen* (two) + ·*ford*. Either, one on a river that has two arms, or perhaps a place where there were two fords side by side on the same river.
Walpole *Walpola*	Pool by the wall. OE *weall* (wall) + *pol* (pool). The Roman bank or wall of the Marshland ring also surrounded **Emneth, Terrington, Tilney,** and **Clenchwarton. Cf. Walsoken, West Walton.**
Walsoken *Walsoca*	The district under particular jurisdiction (soke) by the wall. OE *weall* (wall) + *socn* (soke).
Walton (West) *Waltuna*	Settlement by the wall. OE *weall* (wall) + *tun* (enclosure, settlement, farm). **East Walton** has a different derivation.
Weeting *Wetinga*	Wet place. OE *wæt* (wet).
Whitwell *Witewella*	White spring. OE *hwit* (white) + *well* (spring).

| **Yarmouth** | Mouth of the River Yare. *Yare* + OE |
| *Gernemwa* | *mutha* (mouth). |

See also Helhoughton, Lamas, Sandringham.

Occupations and Unnamed People

Ashmanaugh	The pirate's enclosure. OE *æscmann* (pirate) + *haga* (enclosure). The first element may be a nickname.
Bickerston	Enclosure where a beekeeper lived. OE *bicere*
Bicherstuna	(beekeeper) + *tun* (enclosure, settlement, farm).
Boyland	Possibly boys' (servants', peasants') grove,
Boielund	or *Boia*'s grove. The second element is ON *lundr*. The first element is obscure.
Carleton	Enclosure of the free peasants. OE *ceorl* or
Carletuna	ON *karl* (free peasant) + *tun* (enclosure, settlement, farm). **Forehoe** means 'four mounds' and is near Forehoe Hills. **Rode** was held by Robert de Rode in 1346.
Conisford	King's ford. H. ON *kunungr* (king) + *ford*.
Earlham	The Earl's homestead or Herela's homestead.
Erlham	OE *eorl* (earl) or *Herela* + *ham* (homestead).
Earsham	The earl's homestead. OE *eorl* (earl) + *ham*
Ersam	(homestead).
Fishley	Possibly the fisherman's clearing. The
Fiscele	second element is OE *leah* (wood, grove,

29

clearing). The first element may be OE *fisca* (fisherman).

Honing
Haninga

The people at the hill, rock. OE *han* (rock) + *ingas* (the people of).

Horning
Horninga

The people at the bend. Horning is on a sharp bend of the Bure. OE *horna* (bend) + *ingas* (the people of).

Horningtoft
Horninghetoft

Plot of land belonging to the people of Horning. H. OE *horna* (bend) + *ingas* (the people of) + ON *toft* (plot of land, house, homestead).

Lexham
Lecesham

The leech's (the physician's) homestead. OE *læce* (leech) + *ham* (homestead).

Newton Flotman
Niwetuna

New enclosure belonging to a ferryman. OE *niwe* + *tun* (enclosure, settlement, farm) + *floteman* (ferryman). OE *Floteman* is also used as a personal name in DB.

Reepham
Refham

The bailiff's or reeve's manor. OE *gerefa* (bailiff) + *ham* (homestead).

Swanton
Suanetuna

Herdsman's enclosure. OE *swana* (herdsman) + *tun* (enclosure, settlement, farm). **Morley** was held by Robert de Morli in 1346. **Novers** was held by Milo de Nuiers in 1200. **Abbott** belonged to St. Benet's of Holm Abbey.

Thetford
Tedforda

The people's ford, important ford. OE *theod* (people) + *ford*.

Thorpe
Torp

Hamlet. ON *thorp* (hamlet, secondary settlement). **Abbots** belonged to the Abbots of Bury St. Edmunds. **St. Andrew's** has a church of that name.

Toft Monks
Toft

Site of a house. The settlement contained a small Benedictine Priory which belonged to the Abbey of Préaux in Normandy in 1199. ON *toft* (plot of land, house, homestead).

Walcot
Walecota

Serfs' cottage. OE *walacot.*

Wallington
Wallinghetuna

Farmstead of the dwellers by the wall. OE *weall* (wall) + *ingas* (the people of) + *tun* (enclosure, settlement, farm).

Wellingham
Walnecham

Homestead of the people by the stream. OE *well* (spring) + *ingas* (the people of) + *ham* (homestead).

See also Bodham

✿✿✿✿

General Names

Acre (Castle, South, West)
Acre

Plot of arable land. OE *æcer* (plot of arable land, newly-cultivated ground).

Alburgh
Aldeburga

Old or Alda's mound. OE *ald* (old) or *Alda* + *beorg* (hillock, mound).

Aldborough
Aldeburg

Old fort (possibly used for keeping horses). OE *ald* (old) + *burg* (fortified place).

Aldeby
Aldebuy

Old settlement. H. OE *ald* (old) + ON *by* (settlement, village).

Bircham
Brecham

The settlement by the newly-broken-in ground. OE *bræc* (breach) + *ham* (homestead). In the first instance the name belon-

31

ged to **Great Bircham**. The nearby villages of **Bircham Newton** and **Bircham Tofts** suggest that the expansion of the settlement was still taking place at the end of the Anglo-Saxon period. The first settlement by the newly-broken-in ground was probably a relatively early Anglo-Saxon settlement in a heathy country. **Newton** means 'new enclosure', OE *niwe* + *tun* (enclosure, settlement, farm). **Tofts** means 'a homestead', ON *toft* (plot of land, house, homestead).

Bradenham
Bradeham

Broad river meadow or homestead. OE *brad* (broad) + *hamm* (river meadow) or *ham* (homestead).

Bradfield

Spacious tract of open country. OE *brad* (broad) + *feld* (open land).

Breckles
Breccles

Either meadow or clearing by the newly-cleared land. OE *bræc* (breach) + *læs* (meadow) or *leah* (wood, grove, clearing).

Bridgham
Brugam

Homestead by the bridge. OE *brycg* (bridge) + *ham* (homestead).

Briggate

Probably bridge street. ON *bryggia* (bridge) + ON *gata* (street).

Briston
Burstuna

Possibly settlement in the gap. OE ? *byrst* ('loss' in the sense of 'gap') + *tun* (enclosure, settlement, farm).

Brockdish
Brodise

Brook pasture. OE *broc* (brook) + *edisc* (pasture).

Brooke
Broc

A brook. OE *broc*.

Burgh
Burc

A hill, mound. OE *beorg* (hill, mound).

Burnham *Bruneham*	Homestead by a stream. OE *burna* (stream) + *ham* (homestead). **Overy** means 'across the river', OE *ofer* (over) + *ie* (river).
Caister *Castre*	A Roman camp. The OE *ceaster* is derived from L *castra*.
Congham *Congreham*	Probably settlement at the bend. ?H. The second element is *ham* (homestead). The first element has been the subject of much discussion. Two words have been suggested: ON *kongr* (bend) or ON *kongull* (cluster, usually of grapes). The former seems more likely.
Creake *Kriec*	Rock, cliff. CE (Old Welsh) *creic* (rock, cliff). The place is on a ridge.
Cringleford *Kringelforda*	Ford by the round hill. H. ON *kringla* (a circle) + *ford*.
Crostwick *Crostueit*	Clearing by a cross. H. OE *cros* ON *thveit* (meadow, clearing).
Crostwight *Crostwit*	Identical with **Crostwick**.
Denes	Valley. OE *denu* (valley).
Deopham *Depham*	Deep homestead. OE *deop* + *ham* (homestead).
Dunham *Dunham*	Hill farmstead. OE *dun* (hill) + *ham* (homestead). Gelling notes that north-east of Swaffham there is a splendid, flat-topped 'dun', most of the area being beween 250' and 300' above sea-level.
Dunton *Dontuna*	Hill enclosure. OE *dun* (hill) + *tun* (enclosure, settlement, farm).
Easthaugh	Probably eastern enclosure. OE *east* + *haga* (enclosure).

Easton *Estuna*	Eastern enclosure. OE *east* + *tun* (enclosure, settlement, farm).
Eaton *Ettuna*	Enclosure by a river. OE *ea* (river) + *tun* (enclosure, settlement, farm).
Eccles *Heccles*	A church. The CE *ecles* is derived from the L *ecclesia*.
Edgefield *Edisfelda*	Open land with enclosed pasture. OE *edisc* (park, enclosed pasture) + *feld* (open land).
Fordham *Fordham*	Homestead by a ford. OE *ford* + *ham* (homestead).
Forehoe	Four mounds, barrows. ?H. Either OE *feower* or ON *fjorir* (four) + ON *haugr* (hillock, mound).
Fritton *Fridetuna*	Fenced-in enclosure or village. OE *frittu* (fenced-in) + *tun* (enclosure, settlement, farm).
Greenhoe	Green hill. H. OE *grene* + ON *haugr* (hillock, mound).
Gresham *Gressam*	Grassy homestead. OE *græs* + *ham* (homestead).
Hales *Hals*	Nook or corner of land. OE *halh* (nook, corner of land.
Hainford *Hamforda*	Hedged enclosure by the ford. OE *hægan* (enclosure) + *ford*.
Hardwick *Herdewic*	Herd dairy farm. OE *heord* (herd) + *wic* (dairy farm).
Hingham *Hincham*	High homestead. OE *heah* (high) + *ham* (homestead).
Hoe *Hou*	Hill-spur. OE *hoh* (hill-spur).

Holkham *Holcham*	Homestead in a hollow. OE *holc* (hollow) + *ham* (homestead).
Holme *Holm*	Small island or river meadow. ON *holmr* (island, river meadow).
Holme Hale *Holm*	Small island nook. H. ON *holmr* (island, river meadow) +*halh* (nook, corner of land).
Holt *Holt*	Wood, thicket. OE/ON *holt* (wood, thicket).
Howe *Hou*	Hill or burial mound. ON *haugr* (hillock, mound).
Kirstead	Site of a church. OE *ciricstede* partly Scandinavianized.
Langford *Langaforda*	Long ford. OE *lang* (long) + *ford*.
Langhale *Langahala*	Long nook. OE *lang* (long) + *halh* (nook, corner of land).
Langham *Langaham*	Long homestead. OE *lang* (long) + *ham* (homestead), or see **Longham**.
Langley *Langale*	Long grove. OE *lang* (long) + *leah* (wood, grove, clearing).
Leziate *Lesiet*	Meadow gate. OE *læs* (meadow) + *gæt* (gate).
Lingwood	Bank wood. OE *hlinc* (bank) + *widu* (wood).
Litcham *Licham*	Possibly homestead with an enclosure. OE ?*lycce* (enclosure) + *ham* (homestead).
Lyng *Ling*	Bank, ledge. OE *hlinc* (bank). Gelling notes that the road north-east of **East Dereham** follows the course of the River Wensum, and **Lyng** probably derives its name from a river terrace. It could also come from the

ON word for heather (*lyng*), although this is unlikely.

Mangreen
Manegrena

Commonly-owned grassy place. OE *gemæne* (common land) + *grene* (green).

Marham
Marham

Homestead by the pond. OE *mær* (mere) + *ham* (homestead).

Marsham
Marsam

Homestead by the marsh. OE *mersc* (marsh) + *ham* (homestead).

Merton
Meretuna

Pond enclosure. OE *mere* (pond) + *tun* (enclosure, settlement, farm).

Methwold
Methelwalde

Middle woodland. H. ON *methal* (middle) + OE *wald* (woodland, high forest land, or open upland). **Hythe** means 'a landing-place on a river', OE *hyth*.

Metton
Metune

Enclosure with a meadow. OE *mæd* (meadow) or *maeth* (mowing) + *tun*.

Middleton
Mideltuna

Middle farmstead. OE *middel* (middle) + *tun* (enclosure, settlement, farm).

Modney

Middle island. OE *mid(del)* (middle) + *eg* (island).

Morston
Merstuna

Enclosure on the marsh. OE *mersc* (marsh) + *tun* (enclosure, settlement, farm).

Morton

Enclosure on a moor, barren upland. OE *mor* (moor) + *tun* (enclosure, settlement, farm).

Mulbarton
Molkebertuna

Outlying dairy farm. OE *meolc* (milk) + *beretun* (outlying farm).

Narborough
Nereburh

Possibly fortified place at a narrow pass. OE ? *nere* + *burg* (fortified place). The River Nar is near and the river name is almost certainly derived from the place. *Nere* may be a derivative of OE *nearu* (narrow, in the sense of 'pass').

Narford
Nereforda

Ford at a narrow place. OE *nearu* (narrow) + *ford*.

Necton
Nechetuna

Farmstead on a neck of land, ridge. OE *hnecca* (neck) + *tun* (enclosure, settlement, farm).

Newton
Niwetuna

New enclosure. OE *niwe* + *tun* (enclosure, settlement, farm).

Northwold
Nortwalde

North woodland. OE *north* + *wald* (woodland, high forest land, or open upland).

Norwich
Norvic

Northern dwelling or dairy farm. OE *north* + *wic* (dairy farm).

Outwell

See **Upwell**. OE *ut* (out) + *well* (stream).

Pulham
Pulham

Homestead by the pools or water meadow with pools. OE *pyll* (pool) + *ham* (homestead) or *hamm* (water meadow).

Scole

Temporary hut, shed. ON *skali* (shed).

Semer
Semere

Lake. OE *sæ* (lake) + *mere* (mere).

Sidestrand
Sistran

Wide shore. OE *sid* (wide) + *strand* (shore). Cf. **Overstrand**.

Smallburgh
Smaleburga

Bank settlement on the River Smale. OE *Smale* + *beorg* (hillock, mound). *Smale* is the old name for the River Ant.

Somerton
Somertuna

Summer enclosure (near **Winterton**). OE *sumor* (summer) + *tun* (enclosure, settlement, farm).

Southburgh
Berc

Southern hill. OE *suth* (south) + *beorg* (hillock, mound).

Southery
Sutreia

Southern island. OE *suth* (south) + *eg* (island).

Southmere *Sutmere*	Southern lake. OE *suth* (south) + *mere* (mere).
Southwood *Sudwda*	Southern wood. OE *suth* (south) + *wald* (woodland, high forest land, open upland).
Sporle *Sparlea*	Possibly clearing with an enclosure. OE *spearr* (enclosure) + *leah* (wood, grove, clearing).
Staithe	Landing place on a river. OE *stæth* (landing place, inland port).
Stalham *Stalham*	Either homestead by a pool, or homestead with a stable. OE *stall* (place, stable, stall, pool) + *ham* (homestead).
Stanfield *Stanfelda*	Stony open ground. OE *stan* (stone) + *feld* (open ground).
Stanford *Stanforda*	Stony ford. OE *stan* (stone) + *ford*.
Stibbard *Stabyrda*	Path by a bank. OE *stig* (path) + *byrde* (bank). **Stibbard** is some way from the Wensum, and the name may mean something like 'settlement by the road-side'.
Stockton *Stoutuna*	The second element is *tun* (enclosure, settlement, farm). The first element is either OE *stoc* (place, later religious place, dependent farm) or *stocc* (tree trunk). There are three possible meanings: enclosure with tree trunks, farm belonging to a religious order, farm dwelling made of logs.
Stoke *Stokes*	OE *stoc*. This has three possible meanings: place, religious place, dependent farm. **Stoke Ferry** was a settlement named from a ferry over the River Wissey. **Stoke Holy Cross** is named from the church dedication.

38

Stokesby *Stokesbei*	Settlement village. H. OE *stoc* (place, religious place, dependent farm) + ON *by* (settlement, village).
Stow *Stou*	As with the OE *stoc*, *stow* has several possible meanings: place, inhabited place, holy place, hermitage, monastery. **Stow Bardolph** was a settlement held by William Bardulf in 1244. **Stow Bedon** was held by John de Bidun in 1212.
Stradsett *Strateseta*	Place by a Roman road. H. L *strata* (Roman road) + OE *sæta* (place).
Stratton *Stratuna*	Enclosure by a Roman road. H. L *strata* (Roman road) + *tun* (enclosure, settlement, farm). **Strawless** probably means 'without straw'. **St. Mary** & **St. Michael** were named from the dedication of the churches.
Suffield *Sudfelda*	Southern open land. OE *suth* (south) + *feld* (open land).
Sustead *Sutstede*	Southern place. OE *suth* (south) + *stede* (place).
Sutton *Suttuna*	Southern enclosure. OE *suth* (south) + *tun* (enclosure, settlement, farm).
Syderstone *Scidesterna*	The first element is OE *sid* (broad); the second may be OE *sterne* (stern) or OE *gestreon* (property).
Testerton *Estretona*	Eastern enclosure. OE *æt* (at) + *easterra* (eastern) + *tun* (enclosure, settlement, farm).
Thorpland *Torpaland*	Newly-cultivated land near a hamlet. ON *thorp* (hamlet, secondary settlement) + OE/ON *land* (newly-cultivated ground).
Thwaite *Tuit*	A clearing in a wood, (possibly used as a paddock). ON *thveit* (clearing).

Toftrees *Toftes*	The tofts. ON *toft* (field near a house, homestead).
Tunstall *Tunestalle*	Site of an enclosure. OE *tun* (enclosure, settlement, farm) + *stall* (site).
Tunstead *Tonsteda*	Farmstead. OE *tun* (enclosure, settlement, farm) + *stede* (place).
Upton *Uptune*	Higher settlement. OE *upp* (up) + *tun* (enclosure, settlement, farm).
Upwell *Wella*	Settlement higher up the stream. OE *upp* (up) + *well* (spring). **Outwell** may be the later settlement that sprang up outside the old village.
Walton (East) *Waltuna*	Either settlement in a wood, or settlement on uncultivated moorland (wold). OE *weald* (woodland) + *tun* (enclosure, settlement, farm). **West Walton** has a different derivation.
Warham *Warham*	Homestead by the weir or dam. OE *waru* (weir, dam) + *ham* (homestead).
Waterden *Waterdenna*	Valley with water. OE *wæter* (water) + *denu* (valley).
Welbourne *Walebruna*	Spring, stream. OE *well* (spring) + *burna* (stream).
Wells *Guella*	Springs. OE *well* (spring).
Welney	The River Well. OE *wellan* + *ea* (river).
Wereham *Wigreham*	Possibly homestead by the River Vigora (which may have been an old name of the Wissey). The first element may have been something like *Vigora*, the name of a river in France (now the Vière). The second element is OE *ham* (homestead).

Westbriggs *Wesbruge*	Western bridge. H. OE *west* + *feld* ON *bryggia* (bridge).
Westfield *Westfelda*	Western open land. OE *west* + *feld* (open land).
Weston *Westuna*	West enclosure. OE *west* + *tun* (enclosure, settlement, farm).
Westwick *Westwic*	West dairy farm. OE *west* + *wic* (dairy farm).
Wickhampton *Wichamtuna*	Home farm settlement. OE *wic* (dairy farm) + *ham* (homestead) + *tun* (enclosure, settlement, farm).
Wickmere *Wicmera*	Lake by a dairy farm. OE *wic* (dairy farm) + *mere* (lake).
Wighton *Wistuna*	Farm near a village. OE *wic* (dairy farm) + *tun* (enclosure, settlement, farm).
Winch *Wninc*	Dairy farm with pasture. OE *wynn* (meadow, pasture) + *wic* (dairy farm).
Winterton *Wintretuna*	Enclosure used in winter (near **Somerton**) OE *winter* + *tun* (enclosure, settlement, farm).
Witton *Wittuna*	Settlement near a wood. OE *widu* (wood) + *tun* (enclosure, settlement, farm).
Wood Norton *Nortuna*	Settlement at the north woods. OE *wudu* (woods) + *north* + *tun* (enclosure, settlement, farm).
Woodton W*detuna*	Settlement in the woods. OE *wudu* (woods) + *tun* (enclosure, settlement, farm).
Wootton	Identical with **Woodton**.
Worstead W*rdesteda*	Site of homestead. OE *worth* (enclosure, homestead) + *stede* (place, site of).
Worthing	Open place or yard around a homestead. OE *worthign*.

Places of Particular Interest or Intrigue

Belaugh
Belaga
The second element is OE *haga* (enclosure). The first element is obscure, although some argue that the name means 'funeral pyre enclosure'.

Bylaugh
See **Belaugh**.

Glandford
Glanforda
Merriment ford. OE *gleam* (merriment) + *ford*. Possibly ford where sports/games were held.

Halvergate
Halfriate
The name remains unexplained. The first element may be connected with 'half', but the form is not clear. The second element could be OE *geat* (gate). Ekwall suggests that it could be 'half' and 'heriot', OE *here-geatu*. If this were the case the name would mean 'land for which a half heriot was paid'.

Harpley
Herpelai
Most probably 'clearing with a salt-harp', although 'the harp-player's clearing' is a possibility. Either OE *hearpere* (harp-player) or *hearpe* (salt-harp) + *leah* (wood, grove, clearing).

Letheringsett
Laringeseta
Probably Leodhere's fold. OE *Leodhere* + *geset* (fold). OE *hleothre* (sound, melody) is another explanation of the first element, perhaps alluding to the river. See **Glandford**

Matlask
Matelasc
Ash where meetings (moots) were held. H. OE *mæthel* (moot) + ON *askr* (ash).

Needham
Needy settlement (probably unproductive land). OE *nied* (need) + *ham* (homestead).

Poringland
This should mean 'land of the people of

	Þorr, but no such name is known. OE *þorr* means 'leek'.
Quarles	Circles. Either a round place, or place with
Huerueles	stone circles. OE *hwerflas* (circles).
Ringstead	Circular settlement, or place with stone cir-
Rincsteda	cles. OE *hring* (ring) + *stede* (place).
Runcton	The second element is *tun* (enclosure, settle-
Runghetuna	ment, farm). The first element may be de-
	rived from OE *hrung* (a rung, pole) possibly
	in the sense of a primitive bridge. Settlement
	at the bridge. **Holme** means 'small island
	or river meadow'. H.
Saddlebow	Used in 1198. Possibly originally referred
	to a bridge or piece of land similar in shape
	to a saddlebow.
Thursford	Giant's, demon's ford. OE *thyrs* (giant,
Turesfort	demon) + *ford*.
Weybourne	Possibly felon's stream. OE *wearg* (felon)
Wabrunna	+ *burna* (stream). It may have been a place
	where criminals were drowned.

🐦🐦🐦🐦

Individuals, Families, and Dependants

Alburgh	Either Alda's mound, or old mound. OE
Aldeburga	*Alda* + *beorg* (hillock, mound).
Alby	Ali's settlement. ON *Ali* + *by* (settlement,
Alabei	village).
Alethorpe	Ali's farm, hamlet. ON *Ali* + *thorp* (ham-
Alatorp	let, secondary settlement).

Alpington *Alcmuntuna*	Ahlmund's enclosure. OE *Ahlmund* + *tun* (enclosure, settlement, farm).
Antingham *Antigeham*	Homestead of Anta's people. OE *Anta* + *ingas* (the people of) + *ham* (homestead).
Arminghall *Hameringahala*	Possibly nook of Eanmær's people. OE *?Eanmær* + *ingas* (the people of) + *halh* (nook, corner of land).
Aslacton *Aslactuna*	Aslakr's enclosure. H. ON *Aslakr* + OE *tun* (enclosure, settlement, farm).
Attleborough *Atleburc*	Ætla's hill. OE *Ætla* + *beorg* (hillock, mound).
Attlebridge *Atlebruge*	Ætla's bridge. OE *Ætla* + *brycg* (bridge).
Aylmerton *Almartune*	Æthelmær's enclosure. OE *Aethelmær* + *tun* (enclosure, settlement, farm). The spelling change is due to Norman influence.
Aylsham *Ailesham*	Ægel's homestead. OE *Aegel* + *ham* (homestead).
Babingley *Babinghelea*	The grove of Babba's people. OE *Babba* + *ingas* (the people of) + *leah* (wood, grove, clearing).
Baconsthorpe *Baconstorp*	A hamlet owned by Bacon, a Norman. *Bacon* + ON *thorp* (hamlet, secondary settlement). *Bacon* is originally a nickname from OFr.
Bacton *Bachetuna*	Bacca's enclosure. OE *Bacca* + *tun* (enclosure, settlement, farm).
Bagthorpe	Bakki's hamlet. ON *Bakki* + *thorp* (hamlet, secondary settlement).
Banningham *Banincham*	Homestead of Banna's people. OE *Banna* + *ingas* (the people of) + *ham* (homestead).

Barnham *Bernham*	Beorn's homestead.　OE *Beorn* + *ham* (homestead).
Barningham *Berningeham*	Settlement of Beorn's people. OE *Beorn* + *ingas* (the people of) + *ham* (homestead). **Norwood** means 'lying north of the wood' OE *north* + *wudu* (wood).
Barsham *Barsham*	Bar's homestead.　OE *bar* + *ham* (homestead). Bar means 'boar' and is possibly used as a nickname.
Bawdeswell *Balderswella*	Baldhere's spring.　OE *Baldhere* + *well* (spring).
Bayfield *Baiafelda*	Bæga's open land. OE *Bæga* + *feld* (open land).
Beckham *Becheam*	Beocca's homestead.　OE *Beocca* + *ham* (homestead).
Bedingham *edingaham*	Homestead of Beda's people.　OE *Beda* + *ingas* (the people of) + *ham* (homestead).
Beechamwell *Bicham*	Probably the spring at Bicca's homestead. OE *Bicca* + *ham* (homestead) + *well* (spring).
Beighton *Begetuna*	Beaga's enclosure.　OE *Beaga* + *tun* (enclosure, settlement, farm).
Bessingham *Basingeham*	Homestead of Basa's people.　OE *Basa* + *ingas* (the people of) + *ham* (homestead).
Besthorpe *Besethorp*	Bosi's hamlet.　ON *Bosi* + *thorp* (hamlet, secondary settlement).
Billingford *Billingeforda*	Ford of Billa's people.　OE *Billa* + *ingas* (the people of) + *ford*.
Billockby *Bithlakebei*	The first element may be an unknown ON personal name, or it may be a combination of the ON name *Aki*, prefixed by ON *bithill*

(wooer). The second element is ON *by* (settlement, village).

Bergh Apton
Berc
The hill at Api's farm. H. OE *beorg* (hill or mound) + ON *?Api* + *tun* (enclosure, settlement, farm).

Bexwell
Bekeswella
Beac's spring. OE *Beac* + *well* (spring).

Binham
Binneham
Bynna's homestead. OE *Bynna* + *ham* (homestead).

Bintree
Binnetre
Bynna's tree. OE *Bynna* + *treow* (tree).

Bittering
Britringa
Place of Brihthere's people. OE *Brihthere* + *ingas* (the people of).

Blakeney
Possibly Blaca's island, or black island. OE *Blaca* or *blac* (black) + *eg* (island). The place was previously known as **Snitterley** (DB *Snuterlea*).

Blickling
Blikelinga
Homestead of Blicla's people. OE *Blicla* + *ingas* (the people of).

Bodham
Bodham
Homestead of Boda (a moneyer in DB). OE *Boda* + *ham* (homestead).

Bodney
Bodeneia
Beoda's island. OE *Beoda* + *eg* (island).

Booton
Botuna
Bota's or Bo's enclosure. ?H. OE *Bota* or ON *Bo* + OE *tun* (enclosure, settlement, farm).

Boughton
Buchetuna
Bucca's enclosure. OE *Bucca* + *tun* (enclosure, settlement, farm).

Bowthorpe
Boethorp
Bo's hamlet. ON *Boi* + *thorp* (hamlet, secondary settlement).

Brandiston
Brantestuna
Brant's enclosure. OE *Brant* + *tun* (enclosure, settlement, farm).

Braydeston *Bregestuna*	Brægd's enclosure. OE *Brægd* + *tun* (enclosure, settlement, farm).
Bressingham *Bresingaham*	Homestead of Briosa's people. *Briosa* + *ingas* (the people of) + *ham* (homestead). Briosa means 'gadfly' and may be a nickname.
Brettenham *Bretham*	Bretta's homestead, or possibly homestead of the Britons. OE *Bretta* + *ham* (homestead).
Brinningham *Bruninga*	Homestead of Brina's people. OE *Brina* + *ingas* (the people of) + *ham* (homestead).
Brinton *Bruntuna*	Enclosure of Bryni's people. OE B*ryni* + *ingas* (the people of) + *tun* (enclosure, settlement, farm).
Broomsthorpe *Brunestor*	Brunn's hamlet. ON B*runn* + *thorp* (hamlet, secondary settlement).
Brothercross *Bradescros*	Brothir's cross. ON B*rothir* + *cros* (cross). Perhaps the cross was a memorial.
Buckenham *Bucheham*	Bucca's homestead. OE *Bucca* + *ham* (homestead).
Burlingham *Burlingaham*	Homestead of Bærla's people. OE *Bærla* + *ingas* (the people of) + *ham* (homestead).
Calthorpe *Caletorp*	Kali's hamlet. ON *Kali* + *thorp* (hamlet, secondary settlement).
Cantley *Cantelai*	Canta's (Cantwine) clearing. OE *Canta* + *leah* (wood, grove, clearing).
Caston *Castestuna*	Catt's or Katti's enclosure. OE *Catt* + *tun* (enclosure, settlement, farm). See **Catton**.
Cavick House	Perhaps Cæfic's dairy farm. OE ?*Cæfic* + *wic* (dairy farm).
Catton *Catetuna*	Catta's settlement. OE *Catt* (wild-cat — probably a nickname) + *tun* (enclosure,

settlement, farm).

Cawston
Caustituna

Kalfr's enclosure. H. ON *Kalfr* + OE *tun* (enclosure, settlement, farm). The loss of *l* is due to Norman influence.

Chedgrave
Scatagrava

Ceatta's pit or grove. OE *Ceatta* + either *græf* (pit) or *graf* (grove).

Claxton
Clakestona

Klakkr's enclosure. H. ON *Klakkr* + OE *tun* (enclosure, settlement, farm).

Clenchwarton
Eclewartuna

The enclosure of the people of the Clenc. OE *Clenc* + *waru* (inhabitants) + *tun* (enclosure, settlement, farm). The precise meaning of the first element is obscure — possibly 'lump, mass'.

Clippesby
Clepesbei-

Klyppr's village. ON *Klyppr* + *by* (settlement, village).

Clipston
Clipestuna

Klyppr's enclosure/farm. H. ON *Klyppr* + OE *tun* (enclosure, settlement, farm).

Cockthorpe
Torp

Probably outlying village of Cocc. H. OE *Cocc* + ON *thorp*.

Colby
Colebei

Koli's village. ON *Koli* + *by* (settlement, village).

Colkirk
Colekirka

Koli's or Cola's church. Either OE *Cola* + *cirice*, or ON *Koli* + *kirkia*.

Colney
Coleneia

Cola's island. OE *Cola* + *eg* (island).

Coltishall
Cokershala

Cohede's or Coccede's corner of land. OE *Cohede* or *Coccede* + *halh* (nook, corner of land).

Colton
Coletuna

Koli's settlement. H. ON *Koli* + *tun* (enclosure, settlement, farm).

Colveston
Covestuna

Possibly Kolfr's enclosure. ?H. ON ?*Kolfr* + OE *tun* (enclosure, settlement, farm).

48

Costessey *Costesseia*	Cost's island. OE *Cost* + *eg* (island).
Coston	Karr's enclosure. H. ON *Karr* + *tun* (enclosure, settlement, farm).
Crabhouse	Krabbi's house. ON *Krabbi* + OE/ON *hus* (house).
Cressingham *Cressingaham*	The homestead of Cressa's people. OE *Cressa* + *ingas* (the people of) + *ham* (homestead).
Crimplesham *Crepelesham*	Possibly Crympel's homestead. OE ?*Crympel* + *ham* (homestead). Crympel may be a nickname derived from OE *crump* meaning 'crooked'.
Crownthorpe *Cronkethor*	Possibly Krungla's hamlet. ON ?*Krungla* + *thorp* (hamlet, secondary settlement). Krungla means 'crooked tree' and the word may be descriptive or a nickname.
Croxton *Crokestuna*	Krokr's enclosure. ON *Krokr* + *tun* (enclosure, settlement, farm).
Dalling *Dallinga*	Place of Dalla's people. OE *Dalla* + *ingas* (the people of).
Denver *Danefæla*	Dane's crossing. OE *Dene* + *fær* (passage). Gelling points out that the second element probably went out of use as a name-forming element at an early date and is unlikely to be found in late settlements. A Roman road runs past Denver from Peterborough to the coast. There may have been traffic from Denmark prior to the Viking invasions.
Dersingham *Dersincham*	Homestead of Deorsige's people. OE *Deorsige* + *ingas* (the people of) + *ham* (homestead).

Dickleburgh *Dicclesburc*	Either Dicel's/Dicla's fortified place, or fortified place in the forest clearing belonging to Diss. OE *Dicel/Dicla* or *Dic* + *leah* (wood, grove, clearing) + *burgh* (fortified place).
Didlington *Dudelingatuna*	Enclosure of Duddel's people. OE *Duddel* + *ingas* (the people of) + *tun* (enclosure, settlement, farm).
Dillington	Enclosure of Dylla's or Dylli's people. OE *Dylla/Dylli* + *ingas* (the people of) + *tun* (enclosure, settlement, farm).
Ditchingham *Dicingaham*	Homestead of Dicca's people, or homestead of the dwellers at the dike. OE *Dicca* or *dic* (ditch) + *ingas* (the people of) + *ham* (homestead).
Dunston *Dunestun*	Dunn's enclosure. OE *Dunn* + *tun* (enclosure, settlement, farm).
Edingthorpe	Possibly Eadhelm's secondary settlement. ?H. OE ?*Eadhelm* + ON *thorp* (hamlet, secondary settlement).
Egmere *Egemere*	Ecga's pond. OE *Ecga* + *mere* (lake, pond).
Ellingham *Elingham*	Homestead of Ella's or Eli's people. OE *Ella/Eli* + *ingas* (the people of) + *ham* (homestead).
Elsing *Helsinga*	Place of Elesa's or Ælesa's people. OE *Elesa* or *Ælesa* + *ingas* (the people of).
Erpingham *Erpingaham*	Homestead of Eorp's people. OE *Eorp* + *ingas* (the people of) + *ham* (homestead).
Fakenham *Fachenham*	Facca's homestead. OE *Facca* + *ham* (homestead).

Felmingham *Felmincham*	Homestead of Feolma's/Feolomær's people. OE *Feolma/Feolomær* + *ingas* (the people of) + *ham* (homestead).
Felthorpe *Faltorp*	Fæla's settlement. H. OE *Fæla* + ON *thorp* (hamlet, secondary settlement). Fæla is probably a personal name derived from OE *fæle* meaning 'pleasant'.
Fiddlers Dykes	The family of John Vis de Lu (wolf-face) held the area in 1248. At the time *f* was often pronounced as *v* and there was considerable confusion in the spelling of words which had these letters at the beginning. Words beginning with *v* could be spelt with an *f*. Thus, over time, *Vis de Lu* became *Fiddlers*.
Filby *Filebey*	Possibly Fili's farm or village. ON ?*Fili* + *by* (settlement, village).
Flockthorpe *Flokethorp*	Floki's hamlet. ON *Floki* + *thorp* (hamlet, secondary settlement).
Forncett *Fornesseta*	Forne's or Forni's dwelling-place. OE *Forne* or ON *Forni* + OE *(ge)set* (dwelling-place, fold).
Framingham *Framingaham*	Homestead of Fram's people. OE *Fram* + *ingas* (the people of) + *ham* (homestead). **Earl.** After the Norman Conquest 'Earl' was the usual title for great magnates, in this case the Earl of Norfolk. **Pigot.** Ralph Picot held Framingham Pigot in 1235.
Fransham *Frandesham*	Possibly a name derived from OE *fraemde* or *framede* (strange) + *ham* (homestead).
Freethorpe *Frietorp*	Fræthi's hamlet. ON *Fraethi* + *thorp* (hamlet, secondary settlement).

Frenze	Possibly identical with **Fring** q. v.
Frettenham	Frætta's homestead. OE *Fræta* (a nickname
Fretham	meaning 'wanton') + *ham* (homestead).
Fring	Possibly place of Frea's people. OE ?*Frea*
Frenge	+ *ingas* (the people of).
Fulmodeston	Possibly Fulcmond's enclosure. OE ?*Fulc-*
Fulmotestuna	*mond* + *tun* (enclosure, settlement, farm).
Fundenhall	Possibly Funda's nook. OE ? *Funda* + *halh*
Fundehala	(nook, corner of land).
Garboldisham	Gærbald's homestead. OE *Gaerbald* + *ham*
Gerboldesham	(homestead).
Garveston	Geirulfr's or Gærwulf's enclosure. ?H. ON
Gerolfestuna	*Geirulfr* or OE *Gaerwulf* + *tun* (enclosure,
	settlement, farm).
Gasthorpe	Gaddr's hamlet. ON *Gaddr* + *thorp* (ham-
Gadesthorp	let, secondary settlement).
Gayton	Gæga's enclosure. OE *Gaega* + *tun* (en-
Gaituna	closure, settlement, farm). See **Gaywood**.
	Thorpe. In DB the place is called *Torp*, but
	in 1316 it is recorded as *Aylswithorp* after a
	woman named Æthelswith.
Gaywood	Gæga's wood. OE *Gaega* + *wudu* (wood).
Gaiwde	Gæga may be a nickname derived from OE
	gægan 'to turn aside' (also a river name). Cf.
	Gayton and **Guist**.
Geldeston	Gyldi's enclosure. OE *Gyldi* + *tun* (en-
	closure, settlement, farm).
Gillingham	Homestead of Gylla's people. OE *Gylla* +
Kildincham	*ingas* (the people of) + *ham* (homestead).
Gimingham	Homestead of Gymi's or Gymma's people.
Gimingeham	OE *Gymi/Gymma* + *ingas* (the people of)
	+ *ham* (homestead).

Gissing *Gersinga*	Place of Gyssa's people. OE *Gyssa* + *ingas* (the people of).
Glosthorpe *Glorestorp*	Glor's outlying, dependent enclosure. H. OE *Glor* + ON *thorp* (hamlet, secondary settlement).
Godwick *Goduic*	Goda's dairy farm. OE *Goda* + *wic* (dairy farm).
Gooderstone *Godestuna*	Guthhere's enclosure. OE *Guthhere* + *tun* (enclosure, settlement, farm).
Gorleston *Gorlestuna*	Possibly Gur's enclosure. OE ?*Gur* + *tun* (enclosure, settlement, farm). Gur may be a personal name related to the word for 'girl'.
Gowthorpe *Gheuetorp*	Gaukr's outlying, dependent farm. ON *Gaukr*+*thorp* (hamlet, secondary settlement)
Grimshoe	Grimr's hill. ON *Grimr* + *haugr* (hill),
Grimston *Grimestuna*	Grimr's enclosure. H. ON *Grimr* + *tun* (enclosure, settlement, farm).
Griston *Gristuna*	Gyrdh's or gravelly enclosure. ?H. ON *Gyrdh* or OE *greosn* (gravelly) + *tun* (enclosure, settlement, farm).
Guestwick *Geghestueit*	Clearing belonging to settlement of Guist. 1203 *Geistweit* H. OE *Guist* + ON *thveit* (clearing).
Guiltcross *Gildecros*	Gildi's cross. ON *Gildi* + *cros* (cross). Cf. **Brothercross.**
Guist *Gegeseta*	Gæga's fold or house. OE *Gæga* + either *(ge)set* (fold, dwelling-place) or *sæte* (house).
Gunthorpe *Gunestorp*	Gunni's hamlet. ON *Gunni* + *thorp* (hamlet, secondary settlement).
Gunton *Gunetuna*	Gunni's enclosure. H. ON *Gunni* + OE *tun* (enclosure, settlement, farm).

Haddiscoe *Hadescou*	Haddr's wood. ON *Haddr* + *skogi* (wood).
Hanworth *Haganaworda*	Hagena's enclosure. OE *Hagena* + *worth* (enclosure).
Happisburgh *Hapesburc*	Fort of Hæp's people. OE *Hæp* + *ingas* (the people of) + *burg* (fortified place).
Hapton *Habetuna*	Haba's enclosure. OE *Haba* + *tun* (enclosure, settlement, farm).
Hardingham	Homestead of Heardred's people. OE *Heardred* + *ingas* (the people of) + *ham* (homestead).
Hargham *Herkeham*	Herecca's homestead. OE *Herecca* + *ham* (homestead).
Harleston *Heroluestuna*	Heoruwulf's or Herewulf's enclosure. OE *Heoruwulf*/*Herewulf* + *tun* (enclosure, settlement, farm).
Harling *Herlinga*	Place of Herela's people. OE *Herela* + *ingas* (the people of).
Hassingham *Hasingeham*	Homestead of Hasu's people. OE *Hasu* + *iugas* (the people of) + *ham* (homestead).
Haveringland *Heueringalanda*	Newly-cultivated land of Hæfer's (male goat) people. OE *Hæfer* + *ingas* (the people of) + *land* (newly-cultivated ground).
Heckingham *Hechingheam*	Homestead of Heca's people. OE *Heca* + *ingas* (the people of) + *ham* (homestead).
Hedenham *Hedenaham*	Hedena's homestead. OE *Hedena* + *ham* (homestead).
Helhoughton *Helgetuna*	Helgi's hill-spur settlement. H. ON *Helgi* + OE *hoh* (hill-spur) + *tun* (enclosure, settlement, farm).
Hellesdon *Hailesduna*	Hægel's hill. 985 *Hægelisdun*. OE *Haegel* + *dun* (hill).

54

Hellington
Halgatuna

Identical with **Helhoughton** q.v.

Helmingham
Helmingeham

Homestead of Helm's people. OE Helm + ingas + (the people of) + ham (homestead).

Hemblington
Hemelingetun

Enclosure of Hemele's people. OE Hemele + ingas (the people of) + tun (enclosure, settlement, farm).

Hempnall
Hemenhala

Hemma's nook. OE Hemma + halh (nook, corner of land).

Hempton
Hamatuna

Hemma's enclosure. OE Hemma + tun (enclosure, settlement, farm).

Hemsby
Hemesbei

Possibly Heimir's village. ON ?Heimir + by (settlement, village).

Herringby
Haringebei

Hærringr's village. ON Hærringr + ingas (the people of) + by (settlement, village).

Hevingham
Hevincham

Homestead of Hefa's people. OE Hefa + ingas (the people of) + ham (homestead).

Hickling
Hikelinga

Place of Hicela's people. OE Hicela + ingas (the people of).

Hilborough
Hildeburhwella

Hildeburg's (a woman) enclosure. 1242 Hildenburwrthe. OE Hildeburg + worth (enclosure).

Hilgay
Hidlingheia

Possibly the island of Hythla's people. OE ? Hythla + ? ingas (the people of) + eg (island).

Hillington
Idlinghetuna

Enclosure of Hythla's people. OE Hythla + ingas (the people of) + tnn (enclosure, settlement, farm).

Hindolveston
Hindolfestuna

Hildwulf's enclosure. OE Hildwulf + tun (enclosure, settlement, farm).

Hindringham
Hindringaham

The second and third elements are OE ingas (the people of) + ham (homestead). The

55

first element is obscure, but may be derived from OE *hinder* (behind), in which case the name would mean 'the people dwelling behind', perhaps behind the hills near which the place stands.

Holverston
Holvestuna

Holmfastr's enclosure. H. ON *Holmfastr* + OE *tun* (enclosure, settlement, farm).

Honingham
Hunincham

Homestead of Huna's people. OE *Huna* + *ingas* (the people of) + *ham* (homestead).

Hoveton
Hovetuna

Hofa's enclosure. OE *Hofa* + *tun* (enclosure, settlement, farm).

Hunstanton
Hunestanestuna

Hunstan's enclosure. OE *Hunstan* + *tun* (enclosure, settlement, farm).

Hunworth
Huneworda

Huna's enclosure. OE *Huna* + *worth* (enclosure).

Ickburgh
Iccheburc

Ica's fortified place. OE *Ica* + *burg* (fortified place).

Illington
Illinketuna

Enclosure of Illa's people. OE *Illa* + *ingas* (the people of) + *tun* (enclosure, settlement, farm).

Ingham
Hincham

Inga's homestead. OE *Inga* + *ham* (homestead). Or the first element may be ON *eng* meaning 'river meadow'.

Ingoldisthorpe
Torp

Ingialdr's hamlet. ON *Ingialdr* + *thorp* (hamlet, secondary settlement).

Ingworth
Inghewurda

Inga's enclosure. OE *Inga* + *worth* (enclosure).

Intwood
Intewda

Inta's wood. OE *Inta* + *wudu* (wood).

Irmingland
Erminclanda

The newly-cultivated land of Eorma's people. *Eorma* + *ingas* (the people of) + *land* (newly-cultivated ground).

Islington *Ilsinghetuna*	Enclosure of Elesa's people. OE *Elesa* + *ingas* (the people of) + *tun* (enclosure, settlement, farm).
Itteringham *Ultrincham*	Possibly homestead of Ytra or Ytri's people. OE ?*Ytra/Ytri* + *ingas* (the people of) + *ham* (homestead).
Kelling *Kellinga*	Place of Cylla's people. OE *Cylla* + *ingas* (the people of).
Kempston *Kemestuna*	Cymi's enclosure. OE *Cymi* + *tun* (enclosure, settlement, farm).
Kenninghall *Cheninkehala*	Nook of Cena's or Cyna's people. OE *Cena/Cyna* + *ingas* (the people of) + *halh* (nook, corner of land).
Kenningham	Homestead of Cyna's people. OE *Cyna* + *ingas* (the people of) + *ham* (homestead).
Kerdiston *Kerdestuna*	Cenred's enclosure. OE *Cenred* + *tun* (enclosure, settlement, farm).
Ketteringham *Keterincham*	Homestead of the Cytringas. OE ?*Cuthfrith* + *ingas* (the people of) + *ham* (homestead).
Kettlestone *Ketlestuna*	Ketill's enclosure. H. ON *Ketill* + OE *tun* (enclosure, settlement, farm). Ketill means 'cauldron' and is possibly being used as a nickname for someone round-faced/headed.
Kilverstone *Culvertestuna*	Kilvert's enclosure. OE *Kilvert* + *tun* (enclosure, settlement, farm).
Kimberley *Chineburlai*	Cyneburg's (a woman) clearing. OE *Cyneburg* + *leah* (wood, grove, clearing).
King's Lynn *Lena*	The town almost certainly derived its name from the pool at the mouth of the Ouse. **Lynn** comes from the Celtic *llyn* meaning 'lake'. The town was originally called Lynn, but became Bishop's Lynn because of its

connection with the Bishop of Norwich. Henry VIII's charter of 1537 severed this connection and the name was changed to Lynn Regis (King's Lynn) in honour of the king.

Kipton
Chiptena

Possibly Cyppa's settlement. OE ?*Cyppa* + *tun* (enclosure, settlement, farm).

Kirby
Kerkebei

Village with a church. ON *kirkia* (church) + *by* (settlement, village). **Bedon.** The land was given to Hadenald de Bidun and was held by John de Bidun before 1212. **Cane.** The land was held by Walter de Cadamo in 1205 and by Maria de Cham in 1242. Cane *(Cham)* is a family name derived from **Caen** in France.

Knapton
Kanapatone

Cnapa's enclosure. OE *Cnapa* + *tun* (enclosure, settlement, farm).

Lakenham
Lakemham

Laca's homestead. OE *Laca* + *ham* (homestead).

Larling

Place of Lyrel's people. OE *Lyrel* + *ingas* (the people of).

Lessingham
Losincham

Homestead of Leofsige's people. OE *Leofsige* + *ingas* (the people of) + *ham* (homestead).

Limpenhoe
Limpeho

Limpa's hill-spur. OE *Limpa* + *hoh* (hill-spur).

Longham
Lawingham

Homestead of Lawa's people. OE *Lawa* + *ingas* (the people of) + *ham* (homestead).

Lopham
Lopham

Loppa's homestead. OE *Loppa* + *ham* (homestead).

Ludham
Ludham

Luda's homestead. OE *Luda* + *ham* (homestead)

Mannington *Manninctuna*	Enclosure of Manna's people. OE *Manna* + *ingas* (the people of) + *tun* (enclosure, settlement, farm).
Markshall *Merkeshalle*	Probably Mærec's corner or nook. OE *Mærec* + *halh* (nook or corner of land).
Marlingford *Marthingheforda*	The ford belonging to Mearth's people. OE *Mearth* + *ingas* (the people of) + *ford*. Mearth means 'a marten' and it is possibly used as a nickname. Cf. **Martham.**
Massingham *Masingeham*	Homestead of Mæssa's people. OE *Mæssa* + *ingas* (the people of) + *ham* (homestead).
Mattishall *Mateshala*	Matta's nook. OE *Matta* + *halh* (nook, corner of land.
Mautby *Malteby*	Malti's village. ON *Malti* + *by* (settlement, village).
Melton *Mæltuna*	Middle enclosure. H. ON *methal* (middle) + OE *tun* (enclosure, settlement, farm). **Melton Constable** was held by the Constable of the Bishop of Norwich in 1197.
Mendham *Mendham*	Probably Mynda's homestead. OE ?*Mynda* + *ham* (homestead). Mostly in Suffolk.
Mintlyn *Meltinga*	Possibly Myntel's people. OE M*yntel* + *ingas* (the people of).
Morningthorpe *Maringatorp*	Probably secondary settlement belonging to Mæringas (place of Mæra's people), a lost settlement. H. OE ?*Maeringas* + ON *thorp* (hamlet, secondary settlement).
Moulton *Modetuna*	Moda's enclosure. OE M*oda* + *tun* (enclosure, settlement, farm).
Mundesley *Muleslai*	Mundel's clearing. OE M*undel* + *leah* (wood, grove, clearing).

Mundham *Mundaham*	Munda's homestead. OE *Munda* + *ham* (homestead).
Mundford *Mundeforda*	Munda's ford. OE *Munda* + *ford*.
Neatishead *Snateshirda*	Snæt's household. OE *Snaet* + *hired* (household). The loss of *s* is due to Norman influence.
Norton Subcourse *Nortuna*	The northern enclosure. OE *north* + *tun* (enclosure, settlement, farm). **Subcourse.** Probably from a family name. *Hermannus Sorlecors* is mentioned in 1177.
Oby *Othebei*	Audi's village. ON *Audi* + *by* (settlement, village).
Ormesby *Ormesby*	Ormr's village. ON *Ormr* + *by* (settlement, village).
Osmondiston *Osmondestuna*	Osmond's enclosure. OE *Osmond* + *tun* (enclosure, settlement, farm).
Oulton *Oulstuna*	Outhulf's enclosure. OE *Outhulf* + *tun* (enclosure, settlement, farm).
Ovington	Enclosure of Ufa's people. OE *Ufa* + *ingas* (the people of) + *tun* (enclosure, settlement, farm).
Palgrave *Paggrava*	Paga's grove, copse. OE *Paga* + *graf* (grove, copse).
Palling *Pallinga*	Place of Pælli's people. OE *Pælli* + *ingas* (the people of).
Panxworth *Pankesford*	Panke's ford. OE *Panke* + *ford*.
Pattesley *Patesleia*	Pætti's or Pættel's clearing. OE *Paetti/Pættel* + *leah* (wood, grove, clearing).
Pensthorpe *Penestorpa*	Pening's or Peningr's hamlet. ?H. OE *Pening* or ON *Peningr* + ON *thorp* (hamlet, sec-

ondary settlement).

Pentney
Penteleiet

Penta's island. OE *Penta* + *eg* (island).

Pickenham
Pichenham

Pica's homestead. OE *Pica* + *ham* (homestead).

Postwick
Possuic

Poss's farm. OE *Poss* + *wic* (dairy farm).

Quidenham
Cuidenham

Possibly Cwida's homestead. OE *Cwida* + *ham* (homestead).

Ranworth
Randuorda

Randi's enclosure. H. ON *Randi* + OE *worth* (enclosure). Or the first element may be OE *rand* meaning 'a border' - enclosure with a border.

Raveningham
Raverincham

Homestead of Hræfn's people. OE *Hræfn* + *ingas* (the people of) + *ham* (homestead).

Raynham
Reineham

Regna's homestead. OE *Regna* + *ham* (homestead). Regna is a diminutive form of names such as *Regengar*, *Regnheah*, and *Regnhere*.

Reymerston
Raimerestuna

Possibly Raimer's or Regenmær's enclosure. ?H. ON ?*Raimer* or OE ?*Regenmær* + *tun* (enclosure, settlement, farm).

Riddlesworth
Redelefworda

Hrethel's enclosure. OE *Hrethel* + *worth* (enclosure).

Ridlington
Ridlinketuna

The second and third elements are OE *ingas* (the people of) and *tun* (enclosure, settlement, farm) respectively. The first element may be *hreod* (reedy), *rydde* (cleared), or *Hrethel*. The latter is more likely.

Ringland
Remingaland

Possibly the newly-cultivated land of Rymi's people. OE ?*Rymi* + *ingas* (the people of) + *land* (newly-cultivated land).

61

Rising (Castle & Wood) Either the place of Risa's people, or
Risinga place of people at the brushwood. OE *Risa*
or *hris* (brushwood) + *ingas* (the people of).

Rollesby Hrothulfri's village. ON *Hrothulfri* + *by*
Rotholfuesbei (settlement, village).

Roxham Probably Hroc's homestead. OE *Hroc* +
Rochesham *ham* (homestead).

Rudham Rudda's homestead. OE *Rudda* + *ham*
Rudeham (homestead).

Runton Runi's or Runa's enclosure. OE *Runi/Runa*
Runetuna + *tun* (enclosure, settlement, farm).

Rushall The second element is OE *halh* (nook, cor-
Rivessala ner of land). The first element is almost
certainly a personal name, possibly derived
from OE *hrife* (fierce).

Saham Toney Homestead by the lake. OE *sæ* (lake) + *ham*
Saham (homestead). **Toney.** The land was owned
by the family of a certain Ralph de Toeni,
standard bearer of William I, just after the
Norman occupation.

Sandringham Sandy homestead of Deorsige's people.
Santdersincham 1286 *Santdersicham*. OE *sand* + *Deorsige* +
ingas (the people of) + *ham* (homestead).
Cf. **Dersingham**.

Saxlingham Possibly homestead of Seaxel's people. OE
Saiselingaham ? *Seaxel* + *ingas* (the people of) + *ham*
Saxelingaham (nr. Holt) (homestead).

Saxthorpe Saxi's hamlet. ON *Saxi* + *thorp* (hamlet,
Saxthorp secondary settlement).

Scottow Spur of land belonging to Scots. OE *Scott*
Scotohou + *hoh* (hill-spur). Scott originally meant

'Irishman', but was later applied to Gaels in Scotland.

Scoulton
Sculetuna
Skuli's farm. H. ON *Skuli* + OE *tun* (enclosure, settlement, farm).

Scratby
Scroutbei
Skrauti's village. ON *Skrauti* + *by* (settlement, village).

Sculthorpe
Sculatorpa
Skuli's hamlet. ON *Skuli* + *thorp* (hamlet, secondary settlement).

Seething
Sithinges
Possibly place of Sitha's people. OE ?*Sitha* + *ingas* (the people of).

Sheringham
Silingeham
Homestead of Scira's people. OE *Scira* + *ingas* (the people of) *ham* (homestead).

Shimpling
Simplinga
Place of Scimpel's people. OE *Scimpel* (a nickname derived from the Old German for 'joke') + *ingas* (the people of).

Shingham
Scingham
Homestead of Scene's people. OE *Scene* + *ingas* (the people of) + *ham* (homestead).

Shotesham
Scotessam
The Scot's homestead. OE *Scott* + *ham* (homestead). See **Scottow**.

Shotford
Scotoford
Possibly the Scot's ford. OE *Scott* + *ford* See **Scottow**. If the first element is OE *gescot* and not *Scott* the name means 'toll ford'.

Shropham
Scerpham
The first element, probably a personal name, is obscure. The second element is OE *ham* (homestead).

Sisland
Sislanda
Sige's (Sigeheah's) newly-cultivated land. OE *Sige* + *land* (newly-cultivated ground).

Skeyton
Scegetuna
Skeggi's farm. H. ON *Skeggi* + *tun* (enclosure, settlement, farm).

Snarehill
Snareshul
Snear's hill. OE *Snear* + *hyll* (hill). Snear means 'swift'.

Snetterton *Snetretuna*	Possibly Syntra's farm. OE ?*Syntra* + *tun* (enclosure, settlement, farm).
Snettisham *Snetesham*	Snæt's homestead. OE *Snæt* + *ham* (homestead).
Snoring *Snaringa*	Place of Snear's people. OE *Snear* + *ingas* (the people of). Cf. **Snarehill**.
Spixworth *Spikeswrda*	Either Spic's enclosure, or bacon farm. OE *Spic* (bacon) + *worth* (enclosure).
Sprowston *Sprowestuna*	Sprow's settlement. OE *Sprow* + *tun* (enclosure, settlement, farm).
Stanninghall *Staningehalla*	Nook of Stan's people. OE *Stan* + *ingas* (the people of) + *halh* (nook, corner of land).
Starston *Sterestuna*	Styrr's enclosure. H. ON *Styrr* + OE *tun* (enclosure, settlement, farm). Identical with **Sturston.**
Sturston *Esterestuna*	Identical with **Starston** q.v.
Surlingham *Sutherlingaham*	Southern homestead of Herela's people. OE *suth* (south) + *Herela* + *ingas* (the people of) + *ham* (homestead). Cf. **Harling**.
Swaffham *Suafham*	Homestead of the Swabians. OE *Swæfa* (Suebi in early sources) + *ham* (homestead).
Swainsthorpe *Sueinestorp*	Either Sveinn's hamlet, or the hamlet belonging to the lads. ON *Sveinn* + *thorp* (hamlet, secondary settlement). Sveinn means 'lad'.
Swannington *Sueningatuna*	The enclosure of Sveinn's people. H. ON *Sveinn* + OE *ingas* (the people of) + *tun* (enclosure, settlement, farm). Cf. **Swainsthorpe**.

Swardeston *Suerdestuna*	Sweord's enclosure. OE *Sweord* + *tun* (enclosure, settlement, farm). Sweord means 'sword'.
Tacolneston *Tacoluestuna*	Tatwulf's enclosure. OE *Tatwulf* + *tun* (enclosure, settlement, farm).
Tasburgh *Taseburc*	Tæsa's fort. OE *Tæsa* + *burg* (fort).
Tatterford *Taterforda*	Tathere's ford. OE *Tathere* + *ford*.
Tattersett *Tattessete*	Tathere's place for animals. OE *Tathere* + *(ge)set* (fold, stable).
Terrington *Tilinghetuna*	Possibly the enclosure of Tira's people. OE ?*Tira* + *ingas* (the people of) + *tun* (enclosure, settlement, farm).
Tharston *Therstuna*	Possibly Therir's enclosure. ?H. ON ?*Therir* + OE *tun* (enclosure, settlement, farm).
Thelveton *Telvetuna*	Thialfi's enclosure. H. ON *Thialfi* + OE *tun* (enclosure, settlement, farm).
Themelthorpe	Possibly Thymel's or Thymli's hamlet. ?H. OE *Thymel* or ON *Thymli* + *thorp* (hamlet, secondary settlement). The first elements are names which are possibly derived from the OE word for 'thimble' or the ON word for 'thumb'.
Thompson *Tomestuna*	Tumi's enclosure. H. ON *Tumi* + OE *tun* (enclosure, settlement, farm).
Threxton *Trectuna*	Either Threc's enclosure, or dirty enclosure. OE *Threc* + *tun* (enclosure, settlement, farm). Threc is derived from a word for 'dirt'.
Thrigby *Trikebei*	Thrykki's village. ON *Thrykki* + *by* (settlement, village).

Thurgarton *Turgartuna*	Thorgeirr's enclosure. H. ON *Thorgeirr* + OE *tun* (enclosure, settlement, farm).
Thuxton *Turstanestuna*	Thorstein's enclosure. H. ON T*horstein* + OE *tun* (enclosure, settlement, farm).
Tibenham *Tibenham*	Tibba's homestead. OE *Tibba* + *ham* (homestead).
Tilney	Tila's river or island. OE *Tila* + *ea* (river) or *eg* (island).
Tittleshall *Titeshala*	Tyttel's nook. OE *Tyttel* + *halh* (nook, corner of land).
Topcroft *Topecroft*	Topi's croft. H. ON *Topi* + OE *croft* (small piece of enclosed arable land adjacent to a house).
Tottenhill *Tottenhella*	Totta's hill. OE *Totta* + *hyll* (hill).
Tottington *Tottintuna*	The enclosure of Totta's people. OE *Totta* + *ingas* (the people of) + *tun* (enclosure, settlement, farm).
Trimingham	Possibly homestead of Trymma's people. OE ?*Trymma* + *ingas* (the people of) + *ham* (homestead).
Tuddenham *Tudenham*	Tudda's homestead. OE *Tudda* + *ham* (homestead).
Tuttington *Tutincghetuna*	Enclosure of Tutta's people. OE T*utta* + *ingas* (the people of) + *tun* (enclosure, settlement, farm).
Tyby *Tytheby*	Tidhe's village. ON T*idhe* + *by* (settlement, village).
Wacton *Waketuna*	Wacca's enclosure. OE W*acca* + *tun* (enclosure, settlement, farm).
Walsham *Walessam*	Wæl's homestead. OE *Wæl* + *ham* (homestead).

Walsingham *Walsingaham*	Homestead of Wæl's people. OE *Wæl* + *ingas* (the people of) + *ham* (homestead). Cf. **Walsham.**
Watlington	Settlement of Wæcel's or Wacol's people. OE *Wæcel/Wacol* + *ingas* (the people of) + *tun* (enclosure, settlement, farm). Wacol means 'watchful'.
Watton *Wadetuna*	Wada's enclosure. OE *Wada* + *tun* (enclosure, settlement, farm).
Waxham *Wacstanesham*	Either Wægstan's homestead, or settlement by the stone where watch was held. OE *Wægstan* or *Waecce* (watch) + *stan* (stone) + *ham* (homestead).
Weasenham *Wesenham*	Possibly Wissa's homestead, although the first element is obscure. OE ?*Wisa* + *ham* (homestead).
Wendling *Wenlinga*	Place of Wendel's people. OE *Wendel* + *ingas* (the people of).
Whissonsett *Witcingkeseta*	The fold of Wic's people. OE *Wic* + *ingas* (the people of) + *(ge)set* (fold, stable). Cf. **Witchingham.**
Whitlingham *Wislingeham*	Homestead of Wihthelm's people. OE *Wihthelm* + *ingas* (the people of) + *ham* (homestead).
Whitlington	Enclosure of Wihthelm's people. OE *Wihthelm* + *ingas* (the people of) + *tun* (enclosure, settlement, farm).
Wiggenhall *Wigrehala*	Wicga's nook. OE *Wicga* + *halh* (nook, corner of land).
Wimbotsham *Winebotesham*	Winebald's homestead. 1060 *Winesbodesham* OE *Winebald* + *ham* (homestead).

| **Winfarthing** | Wina's quarter part of land. OE W*ina* + |
| *Wineferthinc* | *feorthing* (quarter part). |

Witchingham Homestead of Wic's people. OE W*ic* +
Wicingaham *ingas* (the people of) + *ham* (homestead).
Cf. **Whissonsett**

Wiveton Wife's or Wifa's enclosure. OE *Wife/Wifa*
Wivetuna + *tun* (enclosure, settlement, farm).

Wolferton Wylfhere's settlement. OE *Wylfhere* + *tun*
(enclosure, settlement, farm).

Wolterton Wulfthryth's (a woman) enclosure. OE
Ultretune *Wulfthryth* + *tun* (enclosure, settlement,
farm).

Wood Dalling The wood belonging to Dalla's people. OE
Dallinga *wudu* (wood) + *Dalla* + *ingas* (the people
of).

Wormegay The island of Wyrm's people. OE *Wyrm*
Wermegai + *ingas* (the people of) + *eg* (island).

Wramplingham The second and third elements are OE *ingas*
Wranplincham (the people of) + *ham* (homestead). The
first element is obscure. It is probably a personal name, and may be derived from OE
wramp (twist).

Wreningham Possibly homestead of Wrenna's people.
Urnincham OE ?W*renna* + *ingas* (the people of) *ham*
(homestead). Wrenna means 'wren'.

Wymondham Wigmund's or Wiermund's homestead. OE
Wimundham *Wigmund/Wiermund* + *ham* (homestead).

Yelverton Possibly Geldfrith's enclosure. OE ?*Geldfrith*
Ailvertuna + *tun* (enclosure, settlement, farm).

**See also Bawburgh, Bawsey, Bilney, Boyland, Buxton,
Carleton, Coxford, Earlham, Letheringsett, Newton Flotman, Runham, Rushford, Stow, Swanton, Wroxham.**

Suggested Further Reading

Books on Place-names

Cameron, K. (1961) *English Place-names*, Batsford.   A good general book on the subject.

Ekwall, E. (1960) *The Concise Oxford Dictionary of English Place-names (4th Edition)*, Clarendon Press.   This is the most comprehensive reference book on the subject and gives information on over 10,000 place-names.   It contains full details of early spellings and has entries explaining many Old English and Old Norse elements

Gelling, M. (1984) *Place-names in the Landscape*, Dent.   This book contains up-to-date research on particular landscape terms used in place-names.   It is particularly strong on Old Norse terms.   It is readable and challenges Ekwall in several places.

Harrington, E. (1984) *The Meaning of English Place-names*, Blackstaff Press, Belfast.   If you become hooked on place-names, this is the book to have in the front of the car.   It gives the meaning of over 4,000 names without going into the original language elements or spellings.   You would still need to consult Ekwall when you finish your journey.

Reaney, P. H. (1960) *The Origin of English Place-names*, Routledge & Kegan Paul.   A good general book on the subject.

Room, A. (1985) *A Concise Dictionary of Modern Place-names in Great Britain & Ireland*, Oxford University Press.   This traces the origins of over 1,000 names that have arisen since 1500.

Sandred, K. & Lindstrom, B. (1989) *The Place-names of Norfolk Part One (The Place-names of the City of Norwich)*, English Place-Name Society, Nottingham.   This is the first volume on Norfolk produced by the Place-Name Society.   Other volumes on the county are to follow.   Their publications are extremely detailed and are aimed at an academic readership.

Books containing information about the history of English, with sections on how the invasions influenced the language, and some comment on place-names.

Brown, H. M. (1987) *A Speller's Companion*, Brown & Brown, Keeper's Cottage, Westward, Wigton, Cumbria CA7 8NQ. This small publication contains brief historical information with details about how various invasions affected English spelling. It is well worth the cost of postage.

Burchfield, R. (1986) *The English Language*, Oxford University Press. A detailed introduction to factors influencing the language, written by the editor of the *Supplement to the Oxford English Dictionary*.

Crystal, D. (1989) *The English Language*, Penguin. This very readable book has three chapters which provide the best general introduction to the history of English.

Potter, S. (1950) *Our Language*, Penguin. A detailed introduction to the history of English. It contains a chapter on personal and place-names. The amount of information it contains can seem overwhelming for the general reader. It is worth persevering with.

INDEX

Rushford	17	Shipdham	20	Stoke	38
Rushall	62	Shotesham	63	Stokesby	39
Ruston	17	Shotford	63	Stow	39
Ryburgh	17	Shouldham	27	Stradsett	39
Ryston	17	Shropham	63	Stratton	39
Saddlebow	43	Sidestrand	37	Strumpshaw	27
Saham Toney	9, 11, 62	Sisland	63	Sturston	64
Salhouse	17	Skeyton	63	Suffield	39
Sall	4, 17	Sloley	17	Surlingham	64
Salthouse	26	Smallburgh	37	Sustead	39
Sandringham	1, 62	Snarehill	63	Sutton	39
Santon	3, 26	Snetterton	64	Swaftham	64
Saxlingham	62	Snettisham	64	Swafield	28
Saxthorpe	62	Snoring	64	Swainsthorpe	64
Scarning	27	Somerton	37	Swannington	64
Scole	37	South Acre	31	Swanton	30
Sco Ruston	17	Southburgh	37	Swardeston	65
Scottow	62	Southery	37	Syderstone	39
Scoulton	63	Southmere	38	Tacolneston	65
Scratby	63	Southwood	38	Tasburgh	65
Sculthorpe	63	Sparham	27	Tatterford	65
Sedgeford	17	Spixworth	64	Tattersett	65
Seething	63	Sporle	38	Taverham	28
Semer	37	Sprowston	64	Terrington	65
Setchey	17	Staithe	38	Testerton	39
Shadwell	27	Stalham	38	Tharston	65
Sharrington	27	Stanfield	38	Thelveton	65
Shelfanger	27	Stanford	38	Themelthorpe	65
Shelton	27	Stanhoe	27	Thetford	30
Shereford	27	Stanninghall	64	Thompson	65
Sheringham	61	Starston	64	Thornage	17
Shernborne	27	Stibbard	38	Thornham	18
Shimpling	63	Stiffkey	27	Thorpe	30
Shingham	63	Stockton	38	Thorpland	39
Shipden	20	Stody	20	Threxton	65